W9-ASC-962

Catholicism,
Social Control,
and
Modernization
in
Latin America

Prentice-Hall, Inc., Englewood Cliffs, N.J.

WITHDRAWN

Catholicism,

Social Control,

and

Modernization

in

Latin America

IVAN VALLIER   University of California, Santa Cruz

Burgess
BX
1426.2
.V4
C.2

© 1970 by PRENTICE-HALL, INC.
Englewood Cliffs, N.J.

All rights reserved. No part of
this book may be reproduced in any form
or by any means without
permission in writing from the publisher.

Current printing (last digit):
10 9 8 7 6 5 4 3 2 1

C-13-121079-3
P-13-121053-X

Library of Congress Catalog Card Number: 77-99742

Printed in the United States of America

FOR ROY A. CHEVILLE
FRIEND, EDUCATOR, PATRIARCH

PRENTICE-HALL INTERNATIONAL, INC.
London

PRENTICE-HALL OF AUSTRALIA, PTY. LTD.
Sydney

PRENTICE-HALL OF CANADA, LTD.
Toronto

PRENTICE-HALL OF INDIA PRIVATE LTD.
New Delhi

PRENTICE-HALL OF JAPAN, INC.
Tokyo

WILBERT E. MOORE / NEIL J. SMELSER   Editors

Modernization of Traditional Societies Series

055881 11·15·71

The twentieth century will be called many things by future historians—the Age of Global War, perhaps, the Age of Mass Society, the Age of the Psychoanalytic Revolution, to name a few possibilities. One name that historians certainly will not fail to give our century is the Age of the New Nation. For, evidently, the convulsive emergence of the colonies into independence and their subsequent struggle to join the ranks of the prosperous, powerful, and peaceful is the most remarkable revolution of our time. Taking the world as a whole, men are now preoccupied with no subject more than they are with the travail of the New Nations. The world of the social sciences has been studying the pace of social change in these newly emergent areas, and from time to time has been engaging in technical assistance and even in the giving of advice on high levels of social strategy. Little of this effort has reached publicly accessible form. Though technical treatises abound, and isolated, journalistic reports of distinctly exotic countries are not wanting, college curricula have scarcely reflected either the scientific endeavors or the world-wide revolutions in technology and in political affairs. This series on "Modernization of Traditional Societies" is designed to inform scholars, students, and citizens about the way quiet places have come alive, and to introduce at long last materials on

EDITORIAL FOREWORD the contemporary character of

developing areas into college curricula for the thought leaders of the near future. To these ends we have assembled experts over the range of the social sciences and over the range of the areas of the underdeveloped and newly developing sections of the earth that were once troublesome only to themselves.

We are proud to be participants in this series, and proud to offer each of its volumes to the literate world, with the hope that that world may increase, prosper, think, and decide wisely.

WILBERT E. MOORE
NEIL J. SMELSER

This book is a study of the ways in which a complex religious organization conditions the life and character of total societies. The setting is contemporary Latin America; the focal unit is the Roman Catholic Church. Interdependencies between these two entities are examined in terms of the Church's evolving systems of religious control and their effects on cultural, political, and motivational processes. One of the chief aims of the book is to identify the factors that help to free and disentangle the Church and societies from unfruitful alliances. Argentina, Brazil, Chile, Colombia, and Mexico figure prominently as points of comparative analysis. The more general aim is to further our understanding of the causal roles that religions play in impeding or facilitating modernization.

It is a pleasure to record my gratitude to a number of individuals who have helped to bring this book about. Stephen F. Bayne, Jr., Benjamin Nelson, David L. Sills, and Charles Wagley helped me get the project under way. Several Latin American colleagues—Justin O'Farrell, Ivan Illich, José Nun, Renato Poblete, and Gustavo Perez—have given time and knowledge generously. David E. Apter, Robert N. Bellah, Alex Inkeles, Seymour M. Lipset, and Neil Smelser have aided me in numerous and immeasurable ways. They know well enough what I have in mind. Among the many graduate students who have worked with me on problems of contemporary Catholicism,

PREFACE

I have benefited particularly from the contributions of Thomas C. Bruneau, Antonio Cova, Daniel Krieger, Laurie Needham, and Jean Guy Vaillancourt. Superb clerical and housekeeping services were provided by Ann Marie Berlin, Barbara Bozman, and Cleo Stoker through the Institute of International Studies, University of California, Berkeley. Last but not least, I record my thanks to Vivian, Olivia, and John, wife, daughter, and son respectively, who faithfully and unselfishly allowed me time to do my homework. Though I cite these colleagues, friends, and loved ones in appreciation for their help, the contents of the book remain my sole responsibility.

IVAN VALLIER

Contents

Catholicism,

Social Control,

and

Modernization

in

Latin America

Latin American societies are historical extensions of Western European civilization, yet in the present situation they are also part of the Third World. They face both ways and are caught up in the ferment and turmoil that are bred by these countervailing forces. Even more significant is the fact that Latin America is one of the great, if not the greatest, strongholds of Roman Catholicism in the world. Questions naturally emerge about how this religious base is affecting and will affect the processes of change and modernization. One of the ways into this complex problem is to fasten attention on the Church as an institution, to note its distinctive properties, and to ascertain whether or not its shape and place in these societies are being modified. Is Catholicism changing? If so, what are the implications? Recent observers of Latin America are reporting a changing Church, but the indicators used to identify this new phase vary widely.[1]

[1] For a conceptualization, comparison, and analysis of recent trends, see Ivan Vallier, "Religious Elites: Differentiations and Developments in Roman Catholicism," in *Elites in Latin America* (eds. Seymour M. Lipset and Aldo Solari (New York: Oxford University Press, 1967), pp. 190-232. More descriptive reports are found in William J. Coleman, *Latin-American Catholicism. A Self-Evaluation* (Maryknoll, N.Y.: Maryknoll Publications, 1958); François Houtart and Émile Pin, *The Church and the Latin American Revolution* (New York: Sheed and Ward, 1965); John J. Considine, ed., *The Church in the New Latin America* (Notre Dame, Ind.: Fides Publishers, Inc., 1964); John A. Mackay, "Latin America and Revolution— II, The New Mood in the Churches," *The Christian Century*, LXXXII, No. 47, November 24, 1965, 1439-42; Roberto Aizcorbe, "La Nueva Iglesia de los Pobres," *Primera Plana* (Buenos Aires), IV, No. 198, October 11-17, 1966, 34-41.

CHAPTER ONE

Introduction

1

Some observers call attention to the growth of Catholic service programs, such as vocational schools, credit cooperatives, health clinics, and literacy projects. Others view the Church's efforts toward pastoral renewal, liturgical reforms, and the involvement of the laity as significant. Both the Church's relationships to society and its internal structures are said to be changing. More significant for other observers are the attempts of "revolutionary" groups to break the prevailing power structure of the Church and to transform it into an agent of radical change in society. All of these particular initiatives and positions—social service, liturgical and pastoral, the restructuring of society—are given a broader basis of coherence through the work of progressive bishops and theologians who are revising the cultural and symbolic frameworks of Latin American Catholicism. At these levels the problem of religious identity, the meaning of change in the modern world, and the principles of Christian humanism are foci of inquiry and elaboration.

A number of particular individuals, groups, and places have rapidly become symbols of the "new Church": the late Bishop Manuel Larraín's land-reform project in Talca, Chile; Ivan Illich's Center for Intercultural Formation in Cuernavaca, Mexico; Dom Helder Camara's leadership for social justice and political change in Brazil's Northeast; and the late Camilio Torres's revolt against the Colombian hierarchy, and the impetus this gave to the concept of the "guerrilla Church." These more visible carriers of change and innovation are only the public heroes of an extensive movement of activity embracing local protests against bishops, new lines of ecumenical collaboration, bold revolutionary programs of religio-political action, and decisive attempts to alter the entire concept of the "good Catholic." [2]

[2] The spread of clerical rebellions, protests by radical lay groups, and revolutionary thrusts within the Latin American Church has roots in several distinct matrices: (1) episcopal conservatism, or the reluctance of certain bishops to implement changes proposed in the documents of Vatican II (1962-1965), recent papal encyclicals (such as *Populorum Progressio*, 1967), and the collective statements from episcopal conferences, e.g., those formulated by delegates to the Latin American Bishops' Council held in Medellin, Colombia, August-September, 1968; (2) national political situations, exemplified in the repressive measures of the military regime in Brazil, especially since 1967, and the policies of the Ongania government in Argentina; and (3) broader international issues centering on the power of foreign interests in domestic life, the problems of poverty and injustice among the marginal peoples, and Third World identities. In local conflicts, these three themes tend to become interrelated in extremely complicated ways, so that it is not clear whether the problem is political, religious, or cultural. For details on some recent clashes and disruptions, see "Curas: El Motin de Rosario (Argentina)," *Primera Plana*, No. 326, 25 de marzo de 1969, pp. 8-9; "Au Bresil: La multiplication des incidents témoigne d'une réelle tension," *Informations Catholiques Internationales*, No. 315, 1 Juillet, 1968, pp. 8-10; "Miembros de Iglesia Joven Interumpieron Consagración Obispal (Chile)," *El Mercurio*, May 5, 1969 no page reference available; and "Rome lève l'interdit jeté, pour les

┼ Something is happening, but is it significant? If the referent is the history of the Church in Latin America, then it is clear that a new phase of religious development is under way. Although rebellion, reform, and a pastoral concern for social outcasts are threads that run through the past four and a half centuries of the Church's record, the present era does embody qualitatively different styles and is being projected through radically differet conceptions of the relations between God, Church, man, and society.

If the referent for assessing the new Catholicism in Latin America is the international Church, or important sectors of it, such as the Church in France, Holland, Germany, Italy, or the United States, we observe a mixed pattern. On the one hand, many of the theological concepts and program models that are gaining visibility throughout Latin American Catholicism are imports from Western Europe, especially from France and Belgium. Part of the leading edge of the new Church in Latin America replicates what were new currents in France twenty years ago. This lag is an important consideration, particularly since some of the frameworks that are being picked up by Latin Americans, or brought to these countries by priests from Western Europe, did not fare well in their original settings. But there is another side to the relation of Catholic developments in Latin America to the rest of the Church: alongside the heavy input of imported ideas, another set of indigenous frameworks is beginning to emerge, e.g., the concept of a "revolutionary" Church, propositions about the Christian's use of violence, and a merging of Christian values with socialistic models of civil society.[3] Thus it may be that this new phase will generate, seemingly for the first time in Latin America, an indigenous Christian theology and perhaps an accompanying indigenous model of religious action.

If the referent is national development and modernization in Latin

---

prétres, sur le centre de formation de Cuernavaca (Mexique)," [a report on the Ivan Illich affair], *Informations Catholiques Internationales*, No. 339, 1 Juillet, 1969, pp. 10-11.

[3] Consult Emanuel de Kadt, "Paternalism and Populism: Catholicism in Latin America," *Journal of Contemporary History*, II, No. 4, October, 1967, 89-106; Thomas G. Sanders, "Catholicism and Development: The Catholic Left in Brazil," in *Churches and States: The Religious Institution and Modernization*, ed. Kalman H. Silvert (New York: American Universities Field Staff, Inc. 1967), pp. 81-99; Gonzalo Castillo-Cardenas, "Christians and the Struggle for a New Social Order in Latin America," in *The Religious Situation: 1968*, ed. Donald R. Cutler (Boston: Beacon Press, 1968), pp. 498-517. For specific documents and essays that articulate ideas, strategies, and goals of the radical Catholic position, see Antonio Batista Fragoso, "Evangélico y Justicia Social," *Cuadernos de Marcha* (Montevideo), XVII (1968), 12-20; Jose Comblin, "Notas sobre el Documento Básico para la II Conferencia General del CELAM," *ibid.*, pp. 47-57.

American societies, the picture grows hazy. There is no valid evidence to date that the "new Church" is playing a key role in facilitating national development, economic growth, or educational change. Current knowledge about this critical set of relations is being gradually extended, however, without foundations in systematic comparative research.[4] Although some recent writers claim that progressive sectors of the Church represent new forces for democracy or are facilitating the integration of marginal groups into national life,[5] others hold with equal conviction that the Church remains a central conservative fixture and an outright defender of the status quo.[6] It is unlikely that either of these claims is valid across the board. Given the extensive range of social, economic, and political conditions prevailing in the Latin American countries, it is expected that the conservative and progressive emphases of the Church will also be highly variable. This does not assume that the Church is merely a reflection of context, but rather that a religious system, not unlike other complex organizations, interacts with its situation at many levels, with an exchange of effects in both directions.

Yet the major question remains: What is the bearing of Roman Catholicism on the problems of modernization and change in Latin America? These societies are involved in a critical transition stage between tradition and modernity. Their independence as nations goes back 150 years, but deep and chronic problems characterize collective efforts to facilitate structural change in the political, economic, and educational spheres.[7]

[4] Recent discussions of this relationship are found in Thomas G. Sanders, "Religion and Modernization: Some Reflections," Field Letter (TGS-14) to Richard H. Nolte, Institute of Current World Affairs, New York, New York, August 4, 1968; Richard N. Adams, *The Second Sowing: Power and Social Development in Latin America*, San Francisco, California, Chandler Publishing Company, 1967, pp. 212-22; Ralph C. Beals, *Bureaucratic Change in the Mexican Catholic Church, 1926-1950*, Unpublished Ph.D. Dissertation, University of California, Berkeley, 1966, esp. Chapter I, "Religion and Modernization," pp. 1-20; Frederick B. Pike, "Introduction" in William V. D'Antonio and Frederick B. Pike, eds., *Religion, Revolution, and Reform*, New York, Frederick A. Praeger, Publishers, 1964, pp. 3-24; and Thomas C. Bruneau, "Autonomy and Change in the Brazilian Catholic Church," Ms., 1969.

[5] See, for example, Tad Szulc, *The Winds of Revolution* (New York: Frederick A. Praeger, Inc., 1963), p. 22; Osvaldo Sunkel, "Change and Frustration in Chile," in *Obstacles to Change in Latin America*, ed. Claudio Veliz (London: Oxford University Press, 1965), p. 140; Charles W. Anderson, *Toward a Theory of Latin American Politics*, Occasional Paper No. 2 (Nashville, Tenn.: Vanderbilt University, Graduate Center for Latin American Studies, February, 1964), p. 8.

[6] This more conventional and popular view is expressed, for example, by John Gerassi, *The Great Fear* (New York: The Macmillan Company, 1963), pp. 11-12.

[7] The literature on these topics is extensive. For introductory readings, consult Veliz, ed., *Obstacles to Change in Latin America*; José Nun, "A Latin American Phenomenon: The Middle Class Military Coup," in *Trends in Social Science Research in Latin American Studies* (Berkeley, Calif.: Institute of International Studies,

Many factors play a part in weakening sequences of development and modernization: investment patterns, leadership styles, fragmented party systems, trade arrangements, ethnic cleavages, exceptionally high rates of population growth, the politicization of the military, etc. These specific sources of breakdown and retrogression may be viewed, in turn, as extensions of a distinctive cultural system within which Catholicism holds an extraordinarily important place, both as a system of religious meanings and as an institutional phenomenon.[8] Consequently Roman Catholicism confronts anyone who attempts to fathom the problems and prospects of social change in Latin America.

But in which way is Catholicism to be linked to the ups and downs of Latin America's institutional development? One's first inclination is to draw inferences with reference to the Weberian thesis, which states that certain religious orientations and motivational patterns stimulate disci- ✓ plined secular activity, especially a certain type of economic rationality. By some intuitive juxtaposition of the core religious elements that are associated with the "Protestant Ethic"—individual responsibility, secular orientations, ascetic control—against the core religious elements that constitute Latin American Catholicism—hierarchical control, other-worldliness, sacramental release from sin, etc.—it is clear that the latter does not contain that crucial dynamic base. This perspective leads to the conclusion that Roman Catholicism is not only incapable of generating modern ✓ outlooks but actually functions as a major deterrent. Modernizing elites are thereby faced with the problem of either eliminating Catholicism through political force or by cutting its financial and legal lifelines, or isolating its leaders and militants from the major secular spheres.

A more recent trend in scholarship on religion and social change shifts attention from the direct causal influence of religious orientations on economic rationality and entrepreneurship, or other specific variables related to modernization, to the degrees to which religions possess gen-

---

1965), pp. 55-91; Albert O. Hirschman, ed., *Latin American Issues* (New York: The Twentieth Century Fund, 1961), esp. Albert O. Hirschman, "Ideologies of Economic Development in Latin America," pp. 3-42; Merle Kling, "Toward a Theory of Power and Political Instability in Latin America," *The Western Political Quarterly,* IX, No. 1, March, 1956, 21-35; K. H. Silvert, ed., *Expectant Peoples, Nationalism and Development* (New York: Random House, Inc., 1963), esp. Kalman H. Silvert, "The Costs of Anti-Nationalism: Argentina," pp. 347-72; T. R. Fillol, *Social Factors in Economic Development: The Argentine Case* (Cambridge, Mass.: M.I.T. Press, 1961).

[8] This theme is amplified in Ivan A. Vallier and Vivian Vallier, "South American Society," *International Encyclopedia of the Social Sciences,* ed. David L. Sills, Vol. 15, New York: The Macmillan Company & The Free Press, 1968, pp. 64-77.

eral transformative capacities.[9] This perspective, more representative of Weber's emphasis in his comparative studies of religions, leads to an examination of the roles that religions play in accelerating social pluralism, structural differentiation, the institutionalization of universalistic norms, the emergence of new centers of power other than the central government and bureaucracy, and the consolidation of various types of modern roles. As Eisenstadt states it:

The major emphasis in Weber's work on the sociology of religion in general and on the Protestant ethic in particular is not on direct religious injunctions about different types of economic behavior but on the more general *Wirtschafts-ethik* of each religion—that is, on those broader attitudes inherent in the ethos of each which influence and direct economic motives and activities. . . .

It is necessary to reformulate the problem for general purposes of analysis and particularly for the consequent re-examination of the Weberian thesis . . . to follow him further and to analyze the *transformative* capacities of different religions (or, for that matter, of secular ideologies). By transformative capacity is meant the capacity to legitimize, in religious or ideological terms, the development of new motivations, activities, and institutions which were not encompassed by the original impulses and views.[10]

Eisenstadt proceeds to identify the features of Protestantism that produced general transformative capacities and, thus, changes in the spheres of economic behavior, legal activity, and political life. He then describes some of the conditions under which these religious emphases decrease or increase the strength of institutional change: "The transformative capacities of the Protestant groups," as an instance, "were smallest in those cases in which they attained full powers . . . —when their more totalistic and therefore restrictive impulses became dominant—and in situations in which they became downtrodden minorities.[11]

The application of this broader framework to the relation between religion and social change in the Latin American situation leads to two questions: What relations between Catholicism and society emerged in the early stages of national life in these societies? Second, did any of these patterns generate transformative capacities, or were all basically obstructive to initiatives that carried modernizing dimensions? At this point, only preliminary answers are possible.

[9] This perspective is developed in a recent essay by S. N. Eisenstadt, "The Protestant Ethic in an Analytical and Comparative Framework," in *The Protestant Ethic and Modernization*, ed. S. N. Eisenstadt (New York: Basic Books, Publishers, Inc., 1968), pp. 3-45.
[10] *Ibid.*, pp. 9, 10. Italics in original.
[11] *Ibid.*, p. 15.

The central consideration in answering the first question is the relationship of Roman Catholicism to the polity. The independence movement of 1810–1830, which led to the emergence of national states, did not break the institutional monopoly of the Church in the religious sphere, nor did it carry through legal provisions for the separation of Church and state. In fact, the Church was characteristically defined as the official religion of the new nations, and provided special privileges: constitutional support, educational prerogatives, and control over ecclesiastical properties.[12] This meant that the formal power structure at the societal level remained traditional; moreover, that impulses toward pluralism, subsystem autonomy, and aspirations for new types of prestige and status remained tied to pre-independence frameworks.

These configurations grew out of many contemporary factors, external and internal, yet it is relatively clear that part of the pressure for this traditional continuity in the power structure came from Church leaders who realized that Catholic dominance could not be maintained on other than a political basis. The internal life of the Church was weak, the allegiances and orientations of the people were relatively shallow or tied in multiple ways to particularistic themes, and the clergy tended to be highly politicized, rather than defining their roles as spiritual leaders of the people. Because of the special historical and institutional conditions that prevailed from the time of the conquest in the sixteenth century up to the independence period, the Church had not consistently pursued policies aimed toward building religious solidarity or the deepening of lay spirituality. Consequently, when basic changes occurred in the political sphere, the Church did not possess bases of autonomous religious strength. It could not resist the strategy of realigning itself with political power, and turned energetically to the task of securing both the legal bases of privilege and the support of political elites. In short, political guarantees emerged as the basis of adaptive action which, in turn, set into motion a whole range of traditional forms of behavior that are still a central part of the political-religious complex in Latin America.

An answer to the second question—did any of the original patterns generate transformative capacities?—is less complicated. Since the Church did not attempt to establish or work out any new relationships with the central power structure, and thus lost its opportunities for gaining new bases of autonomy and leverage, its religious and symbolic capacities were channeled into directions that perpetuated its special institutional posi-

[12] Historical details on the Church's relations to the polity are examined thoroughly by time period and by country in J. Lloyd Mecham, *Church and State in Latin America. A History of Politico-Ecclesiastical Relations,* rev. ed. (Chapel Hill: The University of North Carolina Press, 1966), first published in 1934.

tion. As the laicist and anticlerical forces began to gain strength, the Church shifted to the side of the conservatives. With the emergence of status groups and anti-Church ideologies that shifted the power away from the conservatives, the Church began to build up its own institutions —trade unions, schools, youth movements, etc.—for the purpose of insulating Catholics from secular influences. These initiatives, in turn, increased the formal power of Church officials over the membership. No less important, Catholics began to rely increasingly on the initiative of Church officials to provide definitions of the situation and to work out appropriate standards of behavior for relating to society. The more the Church became politicized and tied to short-run adaptive strategies, the more the religious and spiritual interests of the rank and file weakened. The Church became a major political actor on behalf of the forces that promised to protect it as an institution, rather than a differentiated religious system with roots in the spiritual life of autonomous membership groups.

This abbreviated, and somewhat selective, description of the institutional trajectory that the Church followed in the postindependence period suggests that the relations between religion and social change are not sufficiently circumscribed by noting the presence or absence of a religion's transformative capacities, since this format produces little more than descriptive statements, e.g., religion X possesses transformative capacities, religion Y does not, and so on. For those who take up the relation between religion and social change in contemporary societies that are bound up with a nontransformative tradition—for example, Latin American societies —the problem must be stated differently: it is to develop concepts and explanatory models that comprehend and give focus to processes by which nontransformative religions either become segregated from modernizing complexes or actually undergo internal changes that give them transformative capacities.

If a society or region inherits a nontransformative religion, does this mean that it is doomed to perpetual stagnation and recurring breakdowns in modernization sequences? Certainly not. First of all, transformative capacities arise out of many sectors of society, not just the religious; second, certain conditions in society may favor a general decline in the strength of the traditional or nontransformative religion or, conversely, favor a "reformation" or inner change in the religion along lines that carry positive consequences for change in the wider society.

The main objective is not simply to ascertain whether or not a religion possesses transformative capacities; it includes the identification of the conditions that help to shift a nontransformative religion toward a transformative position. Are internal factors external factors, or both, critical?

If so, which ones? If a religion undergoes change from a nontransformative position to that of a transformative one, what kinds of interpenetrations occur with society? Along other lines, what kinds of differentiations and structural changes accompany religious change?

THE AIMS OF THE BOOK

The purpose of this book is at least threefold: to identify the major components of contemporary Catholicism in Latin America, to describe the nature of the changes that are taking place in the religious system, and to assess the implications of particular configurations for the processes of change and modernization in society. These objectives are pursued with reference to a specific set of general hypotheses:

1. The traditionalizing effects of Roman Catholicism are not produced primarily by its doctrinal teachings, ritual arrangements, and authority gradations, but by the kinds of structural mechanisms it relies on to achieve and perpetuate religious influence. It is not the content of the beliefs nor the ways in which they define the relation of this world to the other-worldly sphere that lies at the bottom of Catholicism's resistive tendencies, but rather the institutional paths that Church elites have followed in their attempts to preserve a religious monopoly and to insulate the "faithful" from contaminating influences. Organizational and corporate strategies have helped to maintain wider institutional fixes that, in turn, interrupt, deflect, or otherwise reduce modernizing potentialities.

2. The central processes that require attention in the Latin American situation, so far as the relation of Catholicism to social change is concerned, are, first, those that are working to help disengage the Church from traditional involvements in society and, second, those that are helping to foster involvements that facilitate modernization. Processes of extraction or disengagement and processes of realignment or reintegration alike are crucial. These, in turn, involve multiple levels of sociocultural activity. Consequently, the central task is to identify the conditions within the Church and in society that shift the religious system from a traditional style to one that is either neutral to or facilitative of modernizing forces. This means that the first order of business is to study the nature, directions, and conditions of religious system change and then to assess the implications of those changes for trends and initiatives in the modernizing sectors of society.

3. With respect to the types of relational changes that help to shift the Church away from traditional styles of control and influence, none is more important than the process of differentiation that frees both Church and polity from each other. As this occurs, the Church ceases to rely on direct political supports and, concomitantly, the polity or major political groups cease to view the Church as a potential ally and source of legitimation. However, this initial

process of differentiation or autonomization is only a base line from which other developments may take place, e.g., a redefinition of the role of episcopal leaders, the creation of new religio-cultural frameworks, a growth of national centers of religious administration and coordination, a redefinition of the nature of the local church, and a change in the roles of the laymen with regard to the relation between religious and secular roles. All these processes are dependent, at least in part, on the kinds of organizational models progressive elites adopt, the types of ideological–theological frameworks they articulate, and the modes of resocialization they follow in their relations to the laity.

BASIC ASSUMPTIONS AND DEFINITIONS

The discussions of the chapters will be guided by certain assumptions and conceptual sets. I will be speaking, for instance, of the "Catholic system," the "Church," "elites," "developmental models," "mechanisms of influence," "control strategies," and "modes of religious action." These terms reflect an interest in the sociology of problem solving, with special reference to corporate and collective units. They also indicate an interest in organization, power groups, and ideologies. Although it is often advantageous to approach problems of religious change by limiting attention to individuals, giving particular attention to their orientations and motivations, most of the structural and institutional aspects of the religious system are left out. The power and influence that organized groups may play either for or against change, whether the referent is to the religious system itself or to the wider society, are important considerations. Similarly, patterns of authority and decision making, forms of worship and missionary action, and the ways in which new movements are linked to the formal institution may emerge as key variables in a general phase of change. Again, every new conception of religious action carries implications for role relations and may even give rise to a whole range of new collective tendencies. In approaching Latin American Catholicism, these perspectives cannot be neglected.

My intention in working with these themes is to throw light on several central and lingering questions: Is the Church powerful or influential in Latin America? If so, what are the sources of this corporate strength and under what conditions can it be mobilized? If the Church is not strong, what kinds of efforts are being made to improve its bargaining situation? How do the Church's various types of influence affect the wider society? Under what conditions does a Church become politicized? Or depoliticized? Which type of Church is the most susceptible to partisan political involvements: the weak Church or the strong Church? Who are the targets of the "new Church's" programs and initiatives? Are their efforts successful; if so, by what criteria? Do modernization and change in secular society depend on a restricting of the Church's scope of action and public involvements? I make no claim that answers to all these questions can be provided in a short book, nor even in a longer one, since my knowledge does not extend that far. I shall, however, attempt to provide an analytical foundation and a partial empirical base for examining the underlying issues, turning as often as possible to cases and descriptive materials for purposes of illustration and comparison.

Given these selective interests, it may be helpful to define and discuss the major concepts: influence, development, elites, model or strategy, and the Church.

Influence

Influence designates a general and extremely important category of social control, being linked in multiple and subtle ways to other key relational concepts such as power, social pressure, and dominance. Although influence is unequivocally a central focus of sociological analysis, it remains relatively unspecified, possessing multiple referents and serving as a basis for describing many types of structural patterns.[13] Influence is frequently employed as a synonym for power; it is often a corollary of prestige; and it is potentially the product of any office that is institutionalized in a major authority system. Although many explications of the concept have been undertaken recently,[14] little cumulative progress to-

[13] On the problems of translating the concept of influence into measurable items, consult James G. March, "An Introduction to the Theory and Measurement of Influence," *The American Political Science Review*, IL (1955), 431-51; and Dorwin Cartwright, "Influence, Leadership, Control," in *Handbook of Organizations*, ed. James G. March (Chicago: Rand McNally & Co., 1965), pp. 1-47.

[14] Among the many recent formulations, see Robert K. Merton, *Social Theory and Social Structure*, rev., enlarged ed. (Glencoe, Ill.: The Free Press of Glencoe, Inc., 1957), esp. pp. 410-20. Merton examines and classifies the nature of interpersonal influence, its sociological bases, the spheres of its expression, and variables that limit or enlarge its scope.

Robert A. Dahl, in his book *Modern Political Analysis* (Englewood Cliffs, N.J.: Prentice-Hall, Inc., 1963), treats influence as both a general relational concept and, more specifically, as a key aspect of political systems. His clarification of the differences between "influence" and "power" advances possibilities for empirical research.

Two papers by Talcott Parsons, "On the Concept of Influence," *Public Opinion Quarterly*, XXVII, Spring, 1963, 37-62, and "On the Concept of Political Power," *Proceedings of the American Philosophical Society*, CVII, No. 3, June, 1963, 232-62, provide the more advanced reader with a fundamental analysis of the concepts of power and influence and their theoretical significance for the comparative study and analysis of all types of social systems. The paper on "influence," for instance, presents a classificatory scheme that clarifies the relations among a whole set of generalized mechanisms of social interaction, e.g., power, money, the generalization of commitments, and influence.

On "social influence" and the relations between power and influence in organizational change, see Warren G. Bennis, *Changing Organizations* (New York: McGraw-Hill Book Company, 1966), pp. 167-71, 196-98; also J. R. P. French and B. Raven, "The Bases of Social Power," in *Studies in Social Power*, ed. D. Cartwright (Ann Arbor: The University of Michigan Press, 1959), pp. 150-67.

ward a theoretical consensus is being made. Like the now fashionable terms "development," "modernization," "microunit," and "structural differentiation," influence serves many scholarly needs and intellectual styles.

In my judgment, influence should be equated with the capacity of a unit (whether an individual, a group, an association, or a state) to generate commitments—loyalties, resources, behavioral support, etc.—in amounts sufficient to allow the agency of influence to impose a direction of its own choosing on the structure, and thereby to change a situation. An influential is thus a person or corporate unit that is able to place a distinct stamp on a valued sphere of interest or activity. The commitments gained may be of short duration or of a long-standing strength. They remain latent over certain periods, becoming susceptible to activation under certain conditions.

Influence may be gained by either intentional efforts (achieved influence) or accumulated as a byproduct of status, charisma, or other bases of social differentiation. A person who becomes an influential need not have pursued this position intentionally. Or pursuit of influence in one sphere of social life may carry increments of influence in other areas.[15] Merton traces out some of these interrelations as part of his analysis of interpersonal influence and its connections with social stratification.[16] As I attempt to show later on, influence is by no means a unitary phenomenon. There are many types of influence, classifiable by level of relational pattern—interpersonal, intergroup, interorganization, etc.—and by content—ideological influence, status influence, behavioral styles (manner, speech, management of affect), and many other factors. I think that a great deal of the present conceptual and methodological ambiguities surrounding the term influence will be eliminated as steps are taken to separate sources of influence, types of influence, and the conditions under which commitments are gained or latent commitments activated. Each

[15] Influence is centrally relevant to the process of planned change, especially as a resource of the change agent. A recent profile of planned change models gives special attention to the questions of "how and why people are influenced." Bennis proceeds to define power as the "ability to influence" and then breaks power down into five components (all of which can lead to A influencing B):

1. coercive power
2. referent, or identification power (role model)
3. expert power
4. legitimate or traditional power
5. value power.

Bennis then points out, by a process of elimination, that successful change agents rely on type 5. Bennis, *Changing Organizations*, pp. 167-69.
[16] Merton, *Social Theory and Social Structure*, pp. 417-20.

of these analytical foci is directly relevant to the problem of Church influence in Latin America.

Development

Social scientists have readily adopted the concept of development to highlight and clarify certain patterns of change in societies, economies, and political systems.[17] Despite the term's ambiguities, especially with regard to such key concepts as modernization, planned change, and mobilization, "development" possesses a special analytical quality, pointing to the macroscopic changes that change-oriented elites bring about to increase the over-all capacities of a system to meet and deal with its major environments.[18] "Development" thus stands for the upgrading of a system's capacities to absorb change, influence the direction of change, and correspondingly maintain internal cohesion and integration. Huntington, in an extremely valuable essay, formulates the concept of "political development" (in distinction to political modernization) as the "institutionalization of political organizations and procedures" [19] that flow from changes toward greater adaptability, an increase in structural complexity, heightened system autonomy, and the gaining of new levels of internal coherence. Some may claim that this perspective on development is too heavily weighted toward the idea of evolution. If so, the distinction can be easily clarified. Evolution signals broad, macroscopic breakthroughs that occur in the makeup of species or system types over long periods of time.[20] Development, on the other hand, connotes systemic changes

[17] For explicit positions on these vocabularies of social change, see Albert O. Hirschman, *The Strategy of Economic Development* (New Haven: Yale University Press, 1958), Chapters 1 and 2; Reinhard Bendix, *Nation-Building and Citizenship* (New York: John Wiley & Sons, Inc., 1964), pp. 4-15; A. F. K. Organski, *The Stages of Political Development* (New York: Alfred A. Knopf, Inc., 1965), pp. 7 ff; and David E. Apter, *The Politics of Modernization* (Chicago: University of Chicago Press, 1965), p. x; pp. 9 ff.

[18] Systematic, analytical statements on the relation between social units and their environments are found in Talcott Parsons, *Societies: Evolutionary and Comparative Perspectives* (Englewood Cliffs, N.J.: Prentice-Hall, Inc., 1966), pp. 10-16; and Robert A. Rosenthal and Robert S. Weiss, "Problems of Organizational Feedback Processes," in *Social Indicators,* ed. Raymond A. Bauer (Cambridge, Mass.: M.I.T. Press, 1966), pp. 302-40.

[19] Samuel P. Huntington, "Political Development and Political Decay," *World Politics,* XVII, April, 1965, 393.

[20] The concept "evolution" is receiving new currency in theoretical works, e.g., Marshall D. Sahlins and Elman R. Service, eds., *Evolution and Culture* (Ann Arbor: The University of Michigan Press, 1960); Kenneth E. Bock, "Evolution, Function, and Change," *American Sociological Review,* XXVIII, April, 1963, pp. 229-37; and Talcott Parsons, "Evolutionary Universals in Society," *American Sociological Review,* XXIX, June, 1964, 339-57.

that are produced through deliberate efforts in more limited contexts and shorter time spans. Development connotes the adoption of means–ends formulas or rationality, strategic planning, and specialized sequences of a problem-solving nature.

An elite group is an identifiable and fully or partially integrated nucleus of individuals who hold the capacity to exert a decisive influence on a given system's internal processes and its relations to its environments.[21] This influence may be conservative and resistive or innovative and revolutionary. Moreover the means of realizing influence, if potential capacity is turned into action, may vary from the manipulation of symbols, exercising control over scarce resources (wealth, positions, honors), or the formulation of a solution to some problem, to withholding information. Many other particular mechanisms may be employed. Elites may emerge within a structured system on the basis of expert knowledge or through political maneuvering, but usually they arise on the peripheries of an established system.

Within the Church, many specialized elites co-exist. Since my definition of an elite is not equivalent to the incumbents of formally structured leadership statuses, the phrase Church elites cannot be limited to cardinals, bishops, and the higher clergy but must also include laymen and members of the lower clergy who, by virtue of certain behaviors, ideas, personal qualities, or position, possess a capacity for exercising influence or power. The contemporary Latin American Church embraces a wide variety of elite groups: mass media specialists, researchers and planners, militant propagandists, administrative experts, educators, theologians and ideologists, program developers, etc. Within some of these categories one can identify several competing elites, differentiated either by ideological positions or decision-making styles. These elite groups also differ in their relation to the hierarchical nucleus. Some are integral parts of the establishment; others are positioned on the fringes or stand totally alienated from the institutional Church.

Model and Strategy

Officials, emerging elites, and institutional ideologs usually initiate action with reference to a set of plans and objectives. These goals and the

---

[21] This perspective is developed more extensively in Ivan Vallier, "Religious Elites: Differentiations and Developments in Roman Catholicism," in *Elites in Latin America*, pp. 190-232.

procedures that are set up to achieve them, directly or indirectly, embody a set of principles that, in combination, make up a model of action. Thus administrative experts may hold to a bureaucratic model or a human relations model in their daily operations. Missionary specialists may follow a direct evangelical model or an indirect, persuasion model. Those who want to build a new Church may elaborate their plans with reference to the "primitive Church" model, or to that of a modern denomination. In many instances, and especially in times of ferment and innovation, many implicit models of how things should be or how they should be done emerge. Models, thereby, compete, as in a market. The competitive strength of one model over another may have little to do with its intrinsic merits, acceptance being gained on the basis of political considerations or convenience. Sometimes vague models attract more attention than those that are clearly formulated, partly because a vague model can be flexibly related to many particular points of view.

A strategy is a plan of organized action that may or may not flow from an identifiable model. Strategies may involve long time spans or short ones. They may be generated from experience, which is then synthesized, or deduced from a theory. Strategies may be focused on particular clienteles or institutional spheres. All these variations appear in the current activities of Catholic elites.

The Church

To speak of the Church is to call attention to a purposely organized system of religious statuses, articulated norms, and scheduled activities. The Church is a corporate body with definite conceptions of authority, jurisdiction, and system boundaries.[22] Dioceses, for example, headed by bishops with episcopal powers (sacramental, legal, administrative), constitute the "Church" in one respect. Canon law gives each diocesan bishop full powers within his territory. At the same time, the Church is more than a sum of the formal diocesan units. Parochial life, centered around the local church, corporate worship, and pastoral activities, represents another level; so too do the levels of the national Church that come to a focus around the national episcopal conferences and the office of the papal nuncio. Internationally, the Church is a system in every sense of

[22] For a formal description of the juridical, sacramental, and administrative principles of the Roman Catholic Church, see T. Lincoln Bouscaren, Adam C. Ellis, and Francis N. Korth, *Canon Law: A Text and Commentary*, 4th rev. ed. (Milwaukee: The Bruce Publishing Co., 1966).

the word, with extranational structures organized around the office of the Pope and the sacred congregations.[23]

The Church, as a formally established corporate unit, is centered around a sacramentally based system of offices and their occupants: bishops, priests, religious (brothers and sisters), and the more recently restored diaconate.[24] Clustered around these central groups are staff specialists (*periti*), consultants, and militants, who provide the hierarchy with a highly committed and diversified stratum of professional assistance. Each individual encompassed by this "Church system" relies on his religious status as the primary point of reference for all social relations, worldly contacts, and ideological orientations. From the Church these individuals derive rewards and benefits, including a distinct occupational position, a potential if not actual clientele (the rank-and-file members), honorific titles, public deference, and certain measures of material and social security. For these and other reasons, the Church possesses a sociological nature that is distinctive and visible.

Against these formally instituted units stand the connections of the Church to a series of cultural levels: collective world views, broad ethical premises, behavioral codes, and ideologies. No less important, the Church initiates, sponsors, and perpetuates a series of functionally specialized programs: catechistic instruction, a ramified school system, general and specific forms of mass media, as well as sacramentally focused *rites de passage*, communal activities that tie culture and religion into a schedule of public events (*fiestas*), and numerous associations that channel membership loyalties and interests into charitable, apostolic, and social directions.

In its orientations to the world or society, the Church holds manifest and persisting interests that are generated by its sacred mission to reach, teach, and touch with sacramental grace all men.[25] This ambition of universal coverage gives birth to high expectations regarding territorial expansion, the ordering of social behavior and human institutions, and even cultural values along lines reflecting its central beliefs and dogmas. In theological terms, the Church's goal is to lead all men to salvation; in sociological terms, the Church is the instrument for fulfilling this task.

[23] Consult the section, "The Supreme Pontificate and the Hierarchy of the Church," *ibid.*, pp. 152-90.

[24] The restoration of the diaconate was an important focus of deliberation during the sessions of Vatican II. See "Decree on the Missionary Activity of the Church," Art. 16, in *The Documents of Vatican II*, ed. Walter M. Abbott, trans. ed. Joseph L. Gallagher (New York: Guild Press, 1966), p. 605.

[25] Consult the "Dogmatic Constitution on the Church," promulgated by Pope Paul VI on November 21, 1964, *ibid.*, p. 15.

Thus the mainspring of the Church is found in its supernaturally derived obligation to achieve effects and to place its stamp on men and institutions. For these reasons, the Church's relations to society or to specific status groups are best viewed analytically in terms of its nature as a system of intentional and purposeful social control. This is indeed a selective definition, but it bears directly on the nature and consequences of Church influence.

I shall assume for theoretical purposes (although I think it is also valid as an empirical generalization) that the *extent* or level of the Church's aspirations for influence or control is historically constant. The Church of the sixteenth century and that of the twentieth differ considerably, even at the broadest levels, in terms of structural features, ideological preoccupations, notions of membership, and criteria of religious achievement; yet both Churches reveal common preoccupations with universal norms, procedures for implanting them in concrete social groups, and the means of consolidating religious loyalties into stable reserves of commitment.

Although this general level or scope of religious ambitions remains constant, the structural or organizational mechanisms that are developed to realize religious control differ immensely by time period and cultural situation. Arrangements that work well at one time turn out to be institutional fixtures of negative significance in another.

In this connection, at least two problems recur in the evolutionary development of the Church: First, it becomes a victim of its own structures and finds with each new age that many of its energies are needed to throw off traditional forms that stand in the way of adaptation; second, the Church continually seeks by various paths (cooptation of spontaneous religious movements, the creation of new lines of professional specialization, the reinterpretation of basic truths, and the rearrangement of the juridical structure, etc.) to build new systems of influence and control. At one time, it sees fit to isolate those who seek the highest state of religious perfection. At another time, it takes the national state as the principal base of control activities. The aristocracy of the seventeenth century is replaced with the bourgeoisie in the nineteenth and early twentieth centuries. Now it is the poor, the marginal people, and the professionals who draw attention as primary target groups. These problems of generating influence stimulate the Church toward change. Far from being a static and settled system, the Church is actually one of the most innovative and experimental of large-scale organizations, being continuously engaged in the process of sociological construction. It does not, however, usually abandon old units or fixtures but merely builds around them, allowing the old institutions to assume more specialized or symbolic roles.

The prominence and pervasiveness of the Roman Catholic Church in the social fabric of Latin America attests to the strength of its control ambitions and the historical effects of its attempts at influencing men to choose "the way of God." The Church is an "instrument" of tremendous complexity, organized around more than 500 ecclesiastical jurisdictions [26]

[26] The table below provides a total picture of the Latin American Church's formally organized ecclesiastical units.

Circunscripciones Eclesiásticas Que Forman Parte Del Consejo Episcopal Latinoamericano

Territorio	Arqui-dióce-sis	Dióce-sis	Prela-turas N	Vica-riatos A	Pre-fectu-ras	Ad-món. Apost.	Aba-días	Cir-cuns-Ecl.
Antilla Británica	1	3						4
Guayana Británica		1						1
Argentina	12	39						51
Bolivia	2	5	3	6				16
Brasil	31	111	38				1	181
Colombia	6	27	1	10	8			52
Costa Rica	1	3		1				5
Cuba	2	4						6
Chile	4	15	2	2				23
Ecuador	3	7	2	4	4			20
El Salvador	1	4						5
Guatemala	1	6	2			1		10
Haití	1	4						5
Honduras	1	3	1					5
México	11	43	1	1	1			57
Nicaragua	1	4	1	1				7
Panamá	1	3	1	1				6
Paraguay	1	3	3	2				9
Perú	4	14	13	7	1			39
Puerto Rico	1	2	1					4
R. Dominicana	1	3	1					5
Uruguay	1	8						9
Venezuela	3	12	1	4				20
Totales:	90	324	71	39	14	1	1	540

Source: Carlos Alfaro, *Guía Apostólica Latinoamericana (Guide to Apostolic Organizations and Movements in Latin America)* (Barcelona: Editorial Herder, 1965), p. 64.

and 15,745 parishes,[27] and including a multitude of specialized programs,
activities, and associations at every level of social life.[28] On an even
broader level, Latin American societies share, but are not unified by, the
existence of a common "religio-Catholic culture." And interspersed between the formal Church and the more general religious culture stands
a staggering array of Catholic-inspired movements, incipient elite groups,
experimental religiously authored parapolitical programs, educational in-

[27] Alonso reports the following statistics on the number of parishes in the Latin
American Church, showing growth trends for the past twenty years: *

Evolución Del Número De Parroquias

Paises	Absoluta				
	1945	1950	1955	1960	1965
Cuba	191	199	206	210	226
Haití	119	126	142	169	179
R. Dominicana	65	65	84	117	128
Puerto Rico	91	101	111	120	152
México	1871	1904	1937	2143	2464
Guatemala	112	114	137	168	224
Honduras	69	69	70	82	93
El Salvador	103	110	118	139	169
Nicaragua	99	100	85	95	122
Costa Rica	75	81	91	96	119
Panamá	57	54	80	79	103
Colombia	1055	1110	1246	1417	1716
Ecuador	370	425	420	524	563
Perú	318	785	859	904	1028
Bolivia	360	368	361	399	385
Chile	502	544	596	636	703
Argentina	931	1075	1158	1347	1609
Uruguay	117	130	147	165	197
Paraguay	153	151	154	158	197
Brasil	3120	3234	3608	4194	4688
Venezuela	410	465	487	582	680
América Latina	10188	11210	12097	13744	15745

* Adapted from Isidoro Alonso, *Estadísticas Religiosas de América
Latina* (*Religious Statistics for Latin America*) Septiembre, 1966,
Mimeo, Cuadro A 3.

[28] Church organizations in Latin America are identified and described by Alfaro,
Guía Apostólica Latinoamericana, pp. 123-221. Introductory descriptions of Church
associations and movements are found in Considine, ed., *Social Revolution in the
New Latin America,* esp. Chapter 6, Marina Bandeira, "Christian Social Movements
in Latin America," pp. 89-101; and Chapter 9, William C. Doherty, Jr., "Christians
and Workers' Movements," pp. 123-38.

stitutions, and charitable organizations, plus programs for research, political and economic development, communication, and literacy training.

In short, the Church typically pursues deliberate policies and stratagems to make its way among competitive agencies of values and beliefs. While the Church was assured of an established position in society or a high birth rate in the families of the faithful, there was little need to develop specialized instruments of control. Things have changed. Structural interdependencies that looked durable a century ago are now completely broken. As old ties and connections were severed, new groups—such as the industrial proletariat and the technicians—began to make a place for themselves in the economic, political, and ideological spheres. On another level, the parish, heretofore the focus of a fully or partially integrated population with the Church as the center of its symbolic life, lost its identity, its cohesiveness, and thus its broad bases of social control that benefited the Church.

Many observers, both within and outside the Church, have noted and analyzed these changes. But few, if any, have viewed these changes in relation to the distinctive features of the Church as an organized enterprise with high aspirations but limited legitimation. Legitimation refers to the degree to which a corporate group can draw support from the central values of a society. On this point the family and the Church provide an interesting contrast.

The family, meaning the legally established union of husband and wife with their children, is a near-universal social unit. The functions it performs are essential to an on-going society. If it does not meet these functions, some other arrangements must be developed to nurture the child, provide sexual expression, and bestow social identity and status. Because of the family's multiple and basic contributions to human society, it is encouraged, provided with legal protections, and bound into a heavy network of formal and informal controls that are triggered when violations occur. Even though marriages may be legitimately broken and children placed in foster institutions, people who discard a particular family unit soon become involved in another. The pressures, for example, on the divorcée to remarry are so strong and pervasive that the probability of remarriage is nearly 100 percent.

But who needs the Church? Although it is probably valid to state that men in all societies experience religious-type emotions and develop institutions that can provide collective expressions of them, one cannot assume that the Church and its activities are capable of providing universal solutions to these needs. Whereas the family, as a set of statuses, activities, and boundaries, appears to satisfy a set of human needs in a more or less viable and universal way, thus meshing structure and need, it is quite clear that the Church, as a set of beliefs, rituals, and statuses, cannot adequately meet all the religious needs of modern man. If it could play this role, then an almost automatic position of legitimacy in society would be gained. It would be defined and valued as an essential institution, and its position would be reinforced by subtle and multiple sources of social control. Of course, this is not the case. The Church may be recognized by society as a legal entity or as a legitimate value agency; but it remains a private interest group, viewed by many people as non-essential, and considered from a number of friendly and hostile points in society as irrelevant to the solution of religious needs.

There is no intention here to either characterize the Church as just another organization or to claim that it is an absolutely unique system. However, any approach to Latin America must include the Catholic system, and any attempt to catch hold of this "Catholic factor" in Latin America must begin with the Church as a social system, historical and contemporary. In terms of the dimensions mentioned above, the Catholic Church is an extraordinary feature of that continent. Its potential lies along many routes and avenues. Within it, there are possibilities for both universalism and particularism, for both the long reach and the soft touch, for flexibility as well as stability.

The accumulated effects of the Church are interspersed in the warp and woof of Latin America. In these terms, these societies may be viewed as a Catholic-based social order. As Ramos writes of his own Mexico: "The real motivation for our culture, given the nature of our psychic activity since the time of the Conquest, is religiosity. . . . Materially or ideally, the church always occupies a high vantage point." [29] MacKay, thirty years ago, traced out this Catholic-religious theme in Latin American culture as expressed in categories of thought, artistic styles, customs and habits, and even in the writings of the vocal, anticlerical liberals such as Bilbao, Montalvo, Prada, and Rodó. [30] Paz makes the point in another way when he states, "We are a ritual people." [31] Freyre's sociohistorical analysis of Brazil underlines the importance of the Catholic theme: "Brazilian development views as a whole may be considered predominantly Christian. . . . [It is] also Catholic, or a branch of the Latin form of Christianity or civilization." [32] These deep and broad religious dimensions are being increasingly recognized by more recent Latin American

[29] Samuel Ramos, *Profile of Man and Culture in Mexico,* trans. Peter G. Earle (New York: McGraw-Hill Book Company, 1962), pp. 77-78.

[30] John A. MacKay, *The Other Spanish Christ* (New York: The Macmillan Company, 1933).

[31] Octavio Paz, *The Labyrinth of Solitude* (New York: Grove Press, 1961), p. 47.

[32] Gilberto Freyre, *New World in the Tropics* (New York: Alfred A. Knopf, Inc., 1959), pp. 4, 39.

scholars. Morse, in a short comment on social science research on Latin America, brings this whole point into clear focus with these questions:

Should not an inquiry into "voting behavior" presuppose understanding of the relation of conscience to natural law in the Hispano-Catholic tradition? Must not an analysis of "the decision-making process" involve knowledge of the moral function of casuistry in a Catholic society? . . . How seriously have any of us dared require a steeping in St. Thomas Aquinas, Dante, and Suárez for those who would understand Latin America? [33]

√ In short, politics, production, and personal meanings are all indirectly imbued with Catholic dimensions and a redemptive *Weltanschauung*. In the midst of misery, confusion, strife, and disillusionment, these people look for a convincing eschatology and for membership in some beautiful crusade.

SUMMARY STATEMENT

The processes that are involved in institutional change, whether approached in terms of values, education, politics, economics, or religion, are essentially processes of restructuring the bases of control and influence. Thus, to establish that relationships exist between religion and modernization, it is necessary to deal with control structures and the ways in which they are being reshaped. Given this perspective, the central way into the problem of the "role of the Church in society" or its implications for modernization or political development is through the evolutionary and comparative study of its bases, strategies, and structures of influence.

At any one point in time, and in a given social context (national, regional, or continental), the Church works with at least three sets of influence structures: (1) those that were developed in the past, and still form part of its total operations; (2) those that are primary for the situation of the present; and (3) those that are in the process of being formed for newly emerging patterns and problems. All three types become mixed and intertwined with each other, creating internal tensions, giving rise to ambiguous public actions, and holding effects for many extrareligious events and processes. This juxtaposition of influence structures—the old and the new, the worn out and the experimental, the proved and the promising—is fully visible in the contemporary Church, whether one turns to Cuba, Argentina, or Colombia. The products of these internal differences are multiple and elusive, both for the Church itself and for the social arenas with which it is in closest contact.

[33] Richard Morse, "The Two Americas," *Encounter,* XXV, No. 3, September, 1965, 93.

The perspective adopted in this book assigns primary importance to the structural features of the Church, its prevailing sources of influence, and the causal roles these configurations may play in social life. Consequently, attention needs to be turned to traditional Catholicism: the typical features of the established Church, entrenched patterns of belief and practice, and characteristic interdependencies that tie traditional Catholicism to nonreligious spheres. Several questions guide the discussion of this chapter: Is the traditional Church monolithic, tightly organized, and institutionally strong? What kinds of loyalties and sentiments does it have at its disposal? By what means does it maintain visibility and exert influence? How does it typically handle threats and uncertainties? What implications do the traditional Church's problem-solving modes hold for public life? I shall give primary emphasis to typical configurations rather than to particular tendencies and variations.

THE TRADITIONAL [1] CHURCH

Although it is true that the Church, territorially speaking, is coextensive with the whole of Latin America, it does not follow

[1] The term "traditional" does not designate a specific type, but rather a cluster of loosely related styles and emphases that emerge as dominant features of the Church as an institution. As later chapters show, several specific subthemes and tendencies exist within traditional Catholicism.

CHAPTER TWO

Traditional Catholicism: Sources of Influence and Adaptive Styles

that it is an integrated, monolithic, and efficient superstructure. The actual situation is quite the opposite.[2] It is ideologically divided, extensively segmented at the national and diocesan levels, and generally uncoordinated in its administrative and pastoral efforts. Its typical structure is flat and decentralized, rather than hierarchical and bureaucratic. Dioceses, by standards in Western Europe and many parts of North America, are very large in geographical area.[3] Within the dioceses, parishes extend over vast amounts of physical space. Communication and interpersonal contacts between priests and between priests and their bishop are sporadic and infrequent. Bishops, on the whole, administer their dioceses loosely and pursue organizational goals through personalized and informal relationships. Traditional Catholicism, in matters relating to ecclesiastical structure, tends to be a conglomerate of relatively isolated formal units, each one of which is tied up with routine local problems and inherited obligations. Mutual complementarity among units in terms of shared objectives and religious purposes is absent.

It is not difficult to identify some of the conditions that have stimulated these structural patterns. The Catholic religion was planted (perhaps "scattered" is a better term) with great haste, throughout territories of vast proportions. Distances between religious centers were immense—a combined result of clergy shortages and the Church's ambition to cover a whole continent. Even more important, each Church official, whether bishop or priest, has been subjected, during most of the past 450 years,

---

[2] The following generalizations are based on two types of research materials: (1) Written reports that directly or indirectly include references to the corporate behavior of the contemporary Church in problem-solving situations, e.g., Leslie Dewart's report on the Cuban hierarchy's responses to Castro's revolutionary movement; see *Christianity and Revolution* (New York: Herder and Herder, Inc., 1963), esp. Part II, "The Revolution and the Church," pp. 89-185; David E. Mutchler, "Roman Catholicism in Brazil," *Studies in Comparative International Development* (St. Louis, Mo.: Washington University Press, 1965), I, No. 8, pp. 103-17; and John J. Kennedy, *Catholicism, Nationalism, and Democracy in Argentina* (Notre Dame, Ind.: Fides Publishers, Inc., 1958). (2) My own studies in South American countries over the past seven years, which have involved field interviews with members of religious elites and laymen, case studies of Church programs and organizations, participation in Catholic conferences and seminars, and the study of internal reports that identify problems and dilemmas of the Church's organizational life.

[3] A recent study of the formal properties of the Latin American Church reports that approximately one-fourth of the dioceses cover less than 10,000 square kilometers, one-fourth cover 40,000 square kilometers or more (with about 8 percent showing more than 90,000 square kilometers), and approximately one-half of the dioceses, or the remainder, cover between 10,000 and 40,000 square kilometers. See Isidoro Alonso, *La Iglesia en América Latina* (Fribourg, Switzerland: Oficina Internacional de Investigaciones Sociales de FERES, 1964), p. 21. In France, by contrast, the typical size of a diocese is approximately 7000 square kilometers.

to extraecclesiastical controls: [4] civil authorities, wealthy patrons, plantation owners, and political leaders. Thus the locus of reference for churchmen who attempted to initiate religious activities or to develop strategies of religious survival came to be the status groups in the local situation. Since nonreligious elites tended to control and take responsibility for the Church, the clergy looked to them instead of being oriented to the international hierarchy or to other sectors of the priesthood.

The traditional Church, lacking organizational autonomy and being variously bound into the social structure at regional and local levels, has been forced to maintain its position and to achieve its goals through short-run maneuvers, through the forming of political coalitions, and by devising *ad hoc* solutions as problems emerged. Directed, long-range planning and systematic programming within a framework of articulated religious objectives have played minor, inconsequential roles in the adaptive process. Special pleas for added monies, requests for more clergy, petitions for opening new missions—all these essential measures have helped to train the bishops and priests in the fine art of shrewd bargaining. The achievement of an influential Church, when it occurred, was less due to the corporate efforts of churchmen working together than to the capacities of individual Catholic officials to build trust and influence through informal negotiations. Thus, the whole "structure" of the Church, as a problem-solving unit, has tended to develop laterally at each hierarchical level, rather than vertically as a united, centralized system. *Quid pro quos,* informal "contracts," and an observing of the rule of tolerance anchor each traditional religious unit into its social context.

Given these continuously necessary exchanges and encounters with elements in secular society, the Church in Latin America early developed a survival strategy that may be termed "political": i.e., a maximization of short-run gains when conditions are favorable, an exercising of restraint in periods of uncertainty, and an ever-ready willingness to be

[4] For details on the origins and evolution of civil and ecclesiastical relations, see J. Lloyd Mecham, *Church and State in Latin America. A History of Politico-Ecclesiastical Relations,* rev. ed. (Chapel Hill: University of North Carolina Press, 1966). On specific problems of jurisdiction and decision-making autonomy, I have found the following works helpful: Peter Masten Dunne, *Early Jesuit Missions in Tarahumara* (Berkeley and Los Angeles: University of California Press, 1948); Mary C. Thornton, *The Church and Freemasonry in Brazil, 1872-1875. A Study in Regalism* (Washington, D.C.: The Catholic University of America Press, 1948); Gilberto Freyre, *New World in the Tropics* (New York: Alfred A. Knopf, Inc., 1959); John J. Kennedy, *Catholicism, Nationalism, and Democracy in Argentina* (Notre Dame, Ind.: Fides Publishers, Inc., 1958); Frederick B. Pike, ed., *The Conflict Between Church and State in Latin America* (New York: Alfred A. Knopf, Inc., 1964).

inconsistent if the situation demands it.[5] Under these circumstances, the Church, as a potential symbol of stable moral authority, undermined its own function. Autonomous religious goals could not be formulated and specified. Immediate, practical matters in the public sphere took precedence over the creation of theological principles, or ethical codes. The Church's energies were largely consumed by political maneuvering— a fundamental requirement under the conditions. The Jesuits represented the only rationally organized segment of the Church in Spanish America. Small surprise that they were thrown out, the Church being as glad to be rid of them as the civil authorities, landowners, and merchants.

Another important feature of the traditional Catholic Church is its lack of capacity to capture and to "process," via its sacraments and pastoral activities, the religious loyalties of the people. A decided gap grew up over the centuries between the Catholic "Church" and the Catholic "religion." This hiatus soon became institutionalized.[6] Some of the roots of this pattern are found in the priest's integral involvement in and his subordination to nonreligious authority systems. The clergy were viewed as a segment of the Crown's control apparatus, rather than as autonomous, available, and sympathetic counselors who would listen to private problems and hold them in confidence. The critical juncture in this process is the sacrament of confession. If this linkage between priest and people remains undeveloped in the Catholic system, one of the basic meanings of Catholic salvation is lost. The lines of interdependence between Church (clergy) and society were patterned horizontally with civil authorities, not vertically with laymen as Church members. The Church's problem of gaining regular access to religious motivation stands in contrast to the situation in sect-type religions. Members of these groups are totally bound up in the religious system. All their religious conceptions, moral codes, spiritual feelings, and sacred words are related directly to the "church," its teachings, rituals, or history. For these people, an almost one-to-one complementarity exists between the church system and religious motivation. Each side of the relationship reinforces the other.

Latin American Catholicism is the extreme opposite case. The Church

[5] When a religious organization is placed in this kind of situation, its goal activities are heavily influenced by short-run and often contradictory involvements. For an analysis of the relation of short-run goals to political systems, see Talcott Parsons, *Structure and Process in Modern Societies* (Glencoe, Ill.: The Free Press of Glencoe, Inc., 1960), p. 106.

[6] On the relation between the Church's formal sacramental life and the religious habits of the membership, see John A. MacKay, *The Other Spanish Christ* (New York: The Macmillan Company, 1933); William J. Coleman, *Latin-American Catholicism* (Maryknoll, N.Y.: Maryknoll Publications, 1958); and Émile Pin, *Elementos para una Sociología del Catolicismo Latinoamericano* (Fribourg, Switzerland: Oficina Internacional de Investigaciones Sociales de FERES, 1963).

has not been able to gain access to or control over many types of religious inclinations. Many of the members' spiritual needs came to be focused on and satisfied through extrasacramental practices, private devotions, "contracts" with divine personages, and by participating in festive, religiously toned social activities. In short, Latin American Catholicism, although strong in its own way, is typically extrasacramental. Consequently the official Church stands separate from habitual religious practice and has been unable to draw on existing religious loyalties for purposes of fostering ethical and spiritual strength. Out of this disjunctivity a compromise pattern has evolved: The Church continues to carry out its ritual forms while the majority of the members proceed to satisfy their religious needs through indigenous and individualistic frameworks. The priest is not in demand and the churches stand frequently empty even though the mass may be celebrated regularly and correctly.

Thus the parishes may be defined as legitimate ritual centers but they are not the primary religious units. Traditional religious loyalties are grounded in nonecclesiastical units—the family, the community—and along informal lines that bind the members of a particular status group to one another.[7] The primary anchorage points of religion are to be discovered in these extrasacramental, communal units, not in the Catholic Church as a formal association. The loyalties that spring from family, friendships, and class contacts include, foster, and perpetuate these religious sentiments. Consequently, the most relevant religious units for analyzing and understanding traditional Latin American Catholicism are the village, the family, and devotional associations. The priest and his sacraments have tended to be peripheral.

This picture is hard to accept, and I do not exaggerate intentionally. Our tendency is to think of Roman Catholicism as a tight, centralized, authoritarian, monolithic organization—one that is effortlessly efficient in matters of administration, one in which all parts are in full communication, and wherein each step or movement is thoroughly appraised in advance for its social or political implications. In short, we have been content to accept the observations of those who perceive that all Catholic

[7] The Catholic Church is assigned a key integrative role among ethnic and racial groups in the city and region of San Cristóbal de Las Casas in Chiapas, Mexico. Relations between the ladinos and Indians are integrated religiously in terms of the Church's universalistic and egalitarian norms on ethnic and racial issues as well as by ritual kinship on the *compadrazgo*. See Benjamin N. Colby and Pierre L. Van Den Berghe, "Ethnic Relations in Southeastern Mexico," *American Anthropologist,* LXIII, No. 4, August, 1961, esp. 775, 782, 785. For more detailed analyses of the *compadrazgo* or ritual kinship system, see Sidney Mintz and Eric R. Wolf, "An Analysis of Ritual Co-Parenthood (*compadrazgo*)," *Southwestern Journal of Anthropology,* VI, 1950, pp. 341-68; and George M. Foster, "Compadrazgo in Spain and in Spanish America," *Southwestern Journal of Anthropology,* IX, 1953, pp. 1-28.

Churches operate like the late Cardinal Spellman's New York archdiocese. In turning to Latin America it is difficult to realize that Catholicism in the United States is a special variant. The traditional Church throughout Latin America is organizationally weak, hierarchically undeveloped, clumsily coordinated, split internally by special interests and extraecclesiastical pressures, and relatively incapable of using its legal framework as an effective system of command and action. By virtue of its diverse privileges in society, by its historical escape from intense religious competition, and by being able to achieve influence and control without concerted, planned activity, the organizational core has not required refinement, elaboration, and continual strengthening measures.

BASIC MODES OF BELIEF AND PRACTICE

Although the beliefs and practices of Latin American Catholics are expressed in manifold ways, specialized studies repeatedly identify a relatively limited range of basic themes and emphases. Of these, none is more important for present purposes than the varying conceptions about the relation of God to the world. Pin provides a threefold description of "religious visions of the world." [8] The first of these views or visions holds that God is naturally present in the world, being fused with all natural objects. This belief in the deity's or deities' immanent presence relieves man, according to Pin, from placing God in the world; He is already there. Moreover, anything that happens in everyday life can be attributed to this presence. According to Pin, this belief tends to eliminate the notion of secondary causes. It also stimulates a posture of accepting things as they are and reinforces tendencies to submit to fate, to make do, and to adjust to circumstances. Two derivatives of this orientation are identified by Pin: "primitive animism" and "popular providentialism." [9] The first instills fear and in turn a reliance on magic. The second manifestation prompts naïve expectations and petitionary prayers. But neither tendency spurs transformative action in the world. Instead, man adjusts to his situation and accepts suffering as a way of life. According to Pin, "The religion of Latin America is a religion of suffering." [10] This suffering theme, or toleration of misery, is linked in some observers' minds to the typical manner of symbolizing Christ—the dying, bleeding, crucified Savior.

The second "religious vision" of God's relationship to the world that typifies many Latin American Catholics is described by Pin as "God is

[8] Pin, 1963, *ibid.*, Chapter III, "Visiones Religiosas del Mundo," pp. 49-58.
[9] *Ibid.*, pp. 49-50.
[10] *Ibid.*, p. 50.

only present in the formal ritual" of the sacraments.[11] The locus of deity is in the institutional Church, pointing man's religious attentions away from the world and toward the supernatural. The sacred and the profane are sharply segregated. The Church and its functionaries, the priests, possess a monopoly over the means of salvation and access to eternal life. God is a transcendent being: aloof, inaccessible except through prescribed, orthodox means, and without meaning for man's relations with mundane institutions. This dualism breeds ritualism, multiplies prayers, stimulates devotionalism, and fosters alienation from the world. Ritual, rather than problem-solving, action results. Religious inclinations are tied to sacramental formalism instead of being channeled into ethical behavior. Moreover it rewards and encourages a privatist or individualistic value framework, since each person is first and always concerned with fulfilling the requirements for eternal salvation. This religious view predisposes the believer to place supernatural objectives and concerns above things of this world. It does not generate a positive basis of action for the world; the chief concern is to refrain from sins against God.

Beyond these two typical orientations, the first of which is most characteristic of the peasant and rural peoples and the second dominant among the traditional upper classes, Pin identifies a third religious view entitled "the transformative presence of God in the world." [12] God possesses confidence in man and the world and assigns man a responsibility for transforming the world. The problems and disabilities of men are seen as tasks to be solved through cooperative activities and a continual insertion of religious values into human relations. In short, the world is assigned a sacredness and legitimacy that encourages men to realize religious values in the midst of secular involvements. Pin refers to both the liturgical movement and recent papal encyclicals as sources of this outlook.

Behavioral Patterns

The reference earlier to the Church's tenuous access to members through formal sacramental activities is borne out by countless studies on the ritual practices of Latin American Catholics.[13] Weekly participa-

---

[11] *Ibid.*, pp. 52-56.

[12] *Ibid.*, pp. 56-58.

[13] At least two types of data are available on these patterns: (1) Anthropological reports that include specific sections on local religious practices and institutions, e.g., Allen Spitzer, "Aspects of Religious Life in Tepoztlán," *Anthropological Quarterly*, XXX, January, 1957, pp. 1-17; William M. Stein, *Hualcán: Life in the Highlands of Peru* (Ithaca, N.Y.: Cornell University Press, 1961); Andrew H. Whitford, *Two Cities of Latin America: A Comparative Description of Social Classes* (Garden City, N.Y.: Anchor Books, Doubleday & Co., Inc., 1964), pp. 77-78,

tion in the mass and monthly communion are characteristic only of a minority. Actual figures vary, as do the precise measures, but the general level of participation is approximately 10 percent of the baptized members.[14] It tends to be highest for the urban, upper-class women and lowest for the urban, male worker or his rural counterpart. The significance of this typical low participative pattern for present purposes is twofold: First, it means that the Church elites, who may be interested in building up religious loyalties or institutional commitments, cannot rely on the conventional parish services to reach the people. Instead, any attempt to mobilize Catholic sentiment, even in its most elementary form, must be tied to a public issue or to a crisis situation. This suggests that influence derived from the membership is unpredictable, thus predisposing officials to turn to other means.

The second implication of weak ritual involvement is financial. Although the readiness to contribute by participating members is low, those who refrain play no part in financial support, except in payment of fees for sacramental services (weddings, funerals, or special masses). By having to charge fees, the priest reinforces and perpetuates the economic image of the Church. Instead of being able to realize financial solvency on the basis of voluntary contributions, the Church's representatives have to impose a ritual tax. This pattern can even help to preserve the magical outlooks of the peasants and urban poor. So long as the people demand ritual formulas from the priests, they (because of a need for money) respond in kind.

A second behavioral configuration coalesces around devotion to and the worship of saints. This is not an unusual pattern in many Catholic countries, and it appears to be especially prominent in Latin America. Here again, the historical policies of the Church are relevant for explanatory purposes. The aloofness of the clergy from the people and the weakness of catechetical instruction stimulated a recourse to those aspects of the supernatural sphere that were accessible outside the sacraments. God

---

92-93, 148-49, 176-88, and 205 n.; Julian Steward, *et al., The People of Puerto Rico* (Urbana, Ill.: University of Illinois Press, 1956), pp. 84-86, 126-27, 214-15; and Roger Bastide, "Les Deux Catholicisms," in *Les Religions au Brésil* (Paris: Presses Universitaires de France, 1960), pp. 151-74. (2) Studies of parish life or regions that are focused specifically on patterns of religious practice, e.g., François Houtart, "A Missionary Parish in Buenos Aires," *Lumen Vitae*, X, Nos. 2-3, 1955, 323-24; and Julio de Santa, *et al., Aspectos Religiosos del Uruguay* (Montevideo: Centro de Estudios Cristianos de la Federación de Iglesias Evangélicos del Uruguay, 1965).

[14] For a summary of religious practices by country and status groups, see François Houtart and Émile Pin, *The Church and the Latin American Revolution* (New York: Sheed and Ward, 1965), Chapter 14, "The Practice of Religion," pp. 164-76.

and His Church were shunted to the background and replaced by help-ing and forgiving saints. The devotional and orational practices that have grown up around patron saints make up the major portion of Catholic practice. Only the grossest kind of ties exist between these and the formal Church. Consequently, the loyalties involved are relatively unmobilizable for ecclesiastical purposes. Even if they could be turned into corporate capital, they would not be relevant to the kinds of problems that the traditional Church is presently confronting.

These patterns of belief and practice are manifest in various combina-tions according to the status and economic position of individuals and groups. Three configurations warrant attention: [15]

Instrumentalism and dependency. These two emphases are central to "folk Catholicism," which is strongest among the peasants and urban poor. God and the saints, as well as the priest, are approached for help in meeting the exigencies of daily life. The supernatural is accessible and subject to manipulation. Religio-magical beliefs pervade all sectors of social life and affect deeply the ways in which men approach problems, make plans, and explain misfortune. This instrumentalism is accompanied by a generalized dependency on God and his helpers: people conceive of the world as a set of forces emanating from a divine order, prompting a sense of immutability. Things are as they are and little can be done to alter the over-all pattern. The most that is possible is to petition for special favors in relation to immediate problems. The tension between these two levels—the underlying deterministic nature of the world and the possibilities for securing particularistic favors—is fundamental, and produces a series of broad orientational postures: resignation, and also naïve hope.

The priest is typically inaccessible to the rural poor and the lower classes in the city, except for periodic visits to celebrate the mass before a *fiesta* celebration, or at points throughout the year when the priest's blessing of the land, domestic animals, and newly planted crops is needed. He is viewed as a quasi-magician—someone who can help to structure the universe in ways that will favor material outcomes.

Obedience and salvation. These emphases are typical of the "good Catholic" or of the women and adolescent girls from the upper status groups. Obedience is centered around two relationships: the authority of the priest, and the dogmas and doctrines of the Church. The Church and its sacraments, its dogmas, and its priesthood are the references for these Catholics. Salvation, or the assurance of life hereafter, is approached

---

[15] For a more extensive description and comparison of religious postures and action tendencies, see Houtart and Pin, *The Church and the Latin American Revo-lution,* Chapter 15, "Religious Motivations," pp. 177-99.

through sacramental participation, confessing one's sins, and adhering to the formal teachings of the Church. Piety, obedience, and faith are conspicuous byproducts. Priests are looked to for moral guidance as well as for instructions to assist in making decisions related to marriage, voting, helping others, and raising children. Devotional societies and token programs of charity are the main associational corollaries of these orientations. God is defined as accessible only through the priest and the sacraments. He is removed from the world; secular events and involvements are not considered critical for his purposes.

Loyalty and customary interest. These orientations to Catholicism, and the Church, typify the bulk of the Church's membership in Latin America. These attitudes characterize both the cultural Catholic and the nominal Catholic. Beliefs in the hereafter and regular participation in the sacraments are characteristically weak. Priests are viewed in diffuse, negative terms. Thus anticlericalism may be expressed, but few cultural Catholics will openly criticize the Church as a spiritual and sacramental entity.

Churchly interests are exposed mainly in events centering around *rites de passage* for members of the family (baptism, confirmation, marriage, funerals). The primary social corollaries of cultural Catholicism are expressive occasions related to primary group ties and political emotion in crisis situations. Involvements in the scheduled sacramental events in the parish or in specialized associations are minimal. Linkages with the Church's educational system may occur, since many of these cultural Catholics have either spent some time in a Catholic school or will send one or more of their children. These Catholics also assert their identities in crisis situations, especially when the faith or the Church is being publicly threatened or mistreated. Usually their other statuses—occupation, political involvements, social ties—determine behavioral and attitudinal postures.

TRADITIONAL SOURCES OF INFLUENCE AND CONTROL

Although the historical trend is toward a diminution of the traditional Church's visibility and its major privileges, it continues to exhibit, promote, and sustain a complex variety of *relational* patterns with the wider social order.[16] Many of these patterns are inherited, providing the Church

[16] I have been helped in this section by the following background works: León Lopetegui and Félix Zubillaga, *Historia de la Iglesia en la América Española, desde el Descubrimiento hasta Comienzos del Siglo XIX. México. America Central. Antillas* (Madrid: Biblioteca de Autores Cristianos, 1965); Antonio de Egaña, *Historia de la Iglesia en la América Española, desde el Descubrimiento hasta Comienzos del Siglo XIX, Hemisferio Sur* (Madrid: Biblioteca de Autores Cristianos, 1966); Mecham, *Church and State in Latin America*, rev. ed.; and Richard M. Morse, "The Heritage of Latin America" in *The Founding of New Societies*, eds. Louis Hartz, *et. al.* (New York: Harcourt, Brace & World, Inc., 1964), pp. 123-77.

with favorable access to power groups, but not necessarily with influence. Other relational patterns take the form of unplanned interdependencies that link the Church to class groups, sectors of the national political system, or the culture of the indigenes. What is "Church" or "non-Church" in certain instances is difficult to identify, since religious and social elements are variously merged or intertwined in symbiotic forms. The priest in the highlands of Colombia or Brazil's interior may, as an instance, occupy a prominent role of diffuse leadership, being not only ritual agent but judge, political leader, educator, and a point of communication with the outside world.

The Church, at the diocesan, provincial, or national level, often enters into more formal and often short-term "contracts" with non-Church groups or agencies to lend legitimacy to a policy or to serve as added lines of defense against a real or imagined enemy. Informal reports from Latin America link some sectors of the Church with the name of the United States government in the context of Agency for International Development (AID) programs or other forms of assistance where the Church is able to reach certain groups in the population or because it is a reasonably good instrument against the "revolutionary left." Various themes of this type are associated with the traditional Church and are necessarily a part of its relations with society. On other levels, many subtle lines of exchange, reciprocity, and alliance may be distinguished between the Church or its key elites and the "old upper class," the military chiefs, and the rising business groups that are gaining vested interests in the estate and *hacienda* patterns of land ownership.

The Church also holds important ties to a certain minority of Catholics who, as regular participants in sacramental services, are drawn into the central arenas of the clergy's leadership. This ritual access to people, stemming from the Church's functions as a distributor of the sacraments, provides another complex range of ties and contacts.

In this section, I shall identify the traditional Church's typical sources of potential influence in society.

Legal Arrangements: The Basis of "Privilege"

The Church entered Latin America under the protection and sponsorship of the Spanish Crown, becoming one of the main instruments of conquest and a permanent fixture of the entire system of social control. The civil rulers were held responsible for the welfare of the Church and for the Christianization of the indigenous peoples. In turn, the secular rulers expected the Church to support the Crown's policies and to accept certain decisions regarding episcopal appointments, financial arrangements, and the establishment of ecclesiastical jurisdictions. The symbiotic patterns that evolved led, in the era of the independence revolts, to a transference of the civil rulers' rights over the Church to the leaders of the new republics.[17] Throughout Latin America, the Church was "re-established" in various ways, once again becoming a sponsored, protected, and "kept" religious organization.

The traditional Church in contemporary Latin America enjoys various degrees of constitutional support. In some instances, the Catholic faith is recognized as the "religion of the people" or as the "official religion." Other provisions guarantee to the Church certain financial subsidies and formal access to the public schools for purposes of carrying on religious instruction. Concordats between the Holy See and the State operate in places like Colombia to give the Church not only an established position but also full rights to decide, in consultation with the Vatican, its own episcopal appointments. There are many variations on Church–State relations in the twenty republics, with Mexico, Cuba, and Uruguay holding the most extreme disestablishment positions, and Peru, Colombia, and perhaps Venezuela ranged on the established side. But whatever the national differences, the Church possesses a high degree of visibility in the central spheres of institutional life, and is capable of drawing considerable support for its various activities. These leverage points at the national level not only help the Church to acquire resources and important types of access but also give it a series of positions on which bargaining can take place. In those instances where additional amounts of pressure are needed, a series of informal ties and backstops can be activated.

Given this important tradition of interdependencies, it is quite understandable that Church–State relations take on special significance in the study of the Church's relations to society. Too often, however, this Church–State theme monopolizes the issue, leaving other ties and connections aside. In my view, Church–State relations represent only one aspect of a wider range of sociological entanglements and connections. Moreover, the variations within the sphere of Church and State are so great that any single generalization about their implications for influence is impossible. The mere fact of an "establishment" clause or of legal separation tells little. Much depends on whether the establishment principle gives major degrees of control to the government, and how the establishment guarantees the Catholic monopoly. Moreover, important differences are produced in instances of "separation" in terms of how the separation is brought about. The process of separation may take place abruptly and explosively, with new bases of secular control over the

[17] The best source on the Independence period is Mecham, *Church and State in Latin America,* Chapters II and III.

Church being built in; or it may evolve in terms of arrangements and agreements that provide a more complete differentiation, with a resultant autonomy for both spheres.

Some clarification on Church–State patterns may be gained through a formal typology. Using two dimensions as a basis of classification: (1) the degree to which the Church is "established," and (2) the degree of Church autonomy (with respect to its internal affairs), we reach the profile noted in Figure 2.1.

FIGURE 2.1

Types of Church–State Relations

Degree to which the
Church is "established"

		high	low
Degree of Church autonomy over its internal affairs	high	privileged	self-sufficient
	low	frustrated	cautious

"Established" high autonomy. In this type, the Church holds a monopoly position as the primary religious institution; but this protection and support does not give the State's representatives the freedom to rule the Church and to control its high-level appointments. Colombia is the nearest approximation to this type. The Concordat of 1887 guarantees the Church's national ascendancy, but it does not give the State full privileges of the *patronato.*

"Established" low autonomy. Within this type, the Church is defined as the religion of the nation and provided certain degrees of support and legitimation; however, the State insists on the exercise of the *patronato,* especially with regard to nominations for vacant or newly organized sees. The Argentine situation, up to 1966 (at which time the *patronato* arrangement was abolished), exemplified this type.

"Separated" low autonomy. The Church in Mexico illustrates this type very well. The Constitution of 1917, reinforcing and elaborating on the statutes of 1856, pushes the Church into a very complete position of separation, yet also subjects the Church to legislation that places it under the surveillance and (if necessary) control of the government. The Church is separate from the State but does not possess full independence to direct and develop its own affairs.

"Separated" high autonomy. This appears to be one of the more fortunate arrangements. The State and Church agree to go their own ways, each under the obligation to maintain its discipline and to order its own affairs. The Chilean case is the key example.

Of course, Church–State involvements and arrangements are much more complex than the illustrative use of the typology implies. Numerous patterns of *ad hoc* alliance, mutual support, and chronic conflict are to be found across nations, along regional and community lines, and within any society over time.

Structural Access to Centers of Power and Decision Making: Formal and Informal

The ramified nature of the Church and its organized activities, in conjunction with the class ties and status connections its leaders possess, provide a series of bases for access to power centers and channels of potential influence. In many circumstances, churchmen are appointed (or elected) to key positions on governmental committees, to law-making bodies, or to membership on the boards of directors responsible for civic, cultural, health, and educational corporations. These memberships link churchmen to a series of important groups and activities in the secular sphere.

On an informal level, or on bases other than formal membership in organized units, churchmen are often closely linked to certain national elites through birth, schooling, and social acquaintance. In these circumstances, access to information, informal decision-making sequences, and powerful individuals is nearly automatic. Churchmen are "well placed" in power circles on the basis of ascribed or inherited characteristics, making it possible and often convenient for them to rely on these connections for promoting the Church's interests. Patterns of this type are undoubtedly most important at the local level, tending to be relied on when legal and formal membership linkages are restricted or weak.

Broad-scope Participation in the Educational System

Despite some losses of privilege with regard to the educational sphere, the Church remains the dominant private institution in every country's school system, in many instances encompassing all levels, from primary grades through advanced university instruction.[18] This access to the new

[18] The Church is permitted to establish educational institutions in all countries except Cuba and Mexico. In the latter country, formal restrictions set by the Constitution of 1917 have gradually been relaxed. For specific materials on the Church's educational systems and wider social configurations, consult Alejandro Bernal Escobar, *et. al., La Educación en Colombia* (Louvain and Bogotá: Oficina Internacional

generation and to the possibilities of orienting future elites and intellectuals provides the Church with an enormous base for generating identifications and transmitting a particular value system, and for reaching primary groups in society. Although there are some indications that the Church's manifold educational activities do not produce ritually committed Catholics, there is no doubt about their potential for influencing the intellectual and social development of the continent.

Limited Leadership Monopolies

On a quite different plane, the Church frequently possesses limited leadership monopolies over particular groups or territorial areas. This pattern is especially evident in isolated rural villages or among certain Indian communities.[19] The priest or apostolic prefect in charge of a missionary area takes on diffuse leadership roles by virtue of being the only full-time professional in the area, and also because he represents a link between the local situation and the wider society. The clergyman, through either periodic contacts or permanent residence, becomes educator, arbitrator, "political" counselor, and a primary source of information, as well as ritual agent and Church authority. A missionary bishop in Brazil's Amazon region exemplifies this position. The main goals of saving souls, preaching the gospel, and administering the sacraments are interrupted and deflected by problems of physical illness, famine, and illiteracy. These conditions, in part a result of the absence of governmental programs in the area, promote a multi-faceted leadership role for the bishop and his priests. Instead of relating to the people as religious specialists, they become involved as construction workers, educators, agents of credit, as well as through a variety of other public and social roles.[20]

Vast regions of Latin America remain sparsely inhabited, distantly removed from urban centers, and oriented to traditional ways. But no area in Latin America is formally outside the organized jurisdictions of

---

de Investigaciones Sociales de FERES, 1965); Luis Scherz-García, "Relations Between Public and Private Universities," in *Elites in Latin America*, eds. Seymour Martin Lipset and Aldo Solari (New York: Oxford University Press, Inc., 1967), pp. 382-407; "Catholic Schools and a Study on Basic Education," in *The Church in the New Latin America*, ed. John J. Considine (Notre Dame, Ind.: Fides Publishers, Inc., 1964), pp. 64-82; and Gustavo Pérez and Isaac Th. J. Wust, "Private Education in Latin America," in *Social Revolution in the New Latin America*, ed. John J. Considine (Notre Dame, Ind.: Fides Publishers, Inc., 1965), pp. 187-95.

[19] This is emphasized in a recent statement by Orlando Fals Borda, "Violence and the Break-up of Tradition in Colombia," in *Obstacles to Change in Latin America*, ed. Claudio Veliz (London: Oxford University Press, 1965), p. 191.

[20] Frank Bonilla, "A Franciscan Bishopric in the Amazon. Some Contemporary Problems of Brazilian Catholicism," *American Universities Field Staff Reports Service*, VIII, No. 5 (Brazil), 1961, 3.

the Church, even though some territories are defined as missionary fields and thus operate under the direct control of the Sacred Congregation for the Propagation of the Faith in Rome.

Culturally Based Religious Loyalties

Tannenbaum's quotable observation about the colonial period to the effect that the Church was everywhere—even when the priest was absent,[21] still holds for many spheres of Latin American life.[22] Being grounded in custom, tradition, and communal activities, having supervisory and ritual roles in relation to human crises and *rites de passage,* and standing both symbolically and organizationally among the higher reaches of power and control in the society, the Church may be likened to the permanent presence that a parent generates over a person from childhood and perhaps throughout his life, even though physical separation occurs and is often sustained.[23] It does not help much to deal with this polyvalent presence in terms of a "religious mystique," or by reference to family symbolism, such as the Church as Mother. Instead, it is necessary to sort out the sociological bases of this diffuse pervasiveness and to inquire into the relation between these bases and the phenomenon of influence.

Even a few steps to uncover the source of this diffuse presence begin to clarify the issue. First of all, the majority of the adult population has had specific contact with the Church via baptism, some type of religious instruction, and perhaps by receiving the sacrament of confirmation. Sec-

[21] Frank Tannenbaum, *Ten Keys to Latin America* (New York: Council on Foreign Relations, Inc., 1960), p. 57.

[22] This does not mean that the official Church is unconcerned about certain definite signs of membership losses and weakened institutional loyalties. Among these signs are the growth of other religions, such as spiritualism and Protestant Pentecostalism; the increasing articulateness of Catholics who admit a commitment to Christianity but who reject the institutional Church; the growing numbers of priests who resign from their sacerdotal duties; finally, a steady decrease in most countries in priestly vocations. On these problems, consult Candido Procopio de Camargo, *Aspectos Sociológicos del Espiritismo en São Paulo,* Fribourg, Switzerland: FERES, 1961; Emilio Willems, *Followers of the Faith: Culture Change and the Rise of Protestantism in Brazil and Chile,* Nashville, Tennessee: Vanderbilt University Press, 1967; Christian Lalive d'Epinay, *El Refugio de las Masas: Estudio Sociológico Protestantismo Chileno,* Santiago, Chile: Editorial del Pacífico, S. A., 1968; Renato Poblete Barth, *Crisis Sacerdotal,* Santiago, Chile: Editorial del Pacífico, S. A., 1965; "Enquête a Santiago: L'Église ne s'intéresse pas à L'homme," *Informations Catholiques Internationales,* No. 296, September 15, 1967, pp. 19-20; and José Marins, "Pesquisa Sôbre o Clero do Brasil," *Revista Eclesiástica Brasileira,* 29, 1, March 31, 1969, pp. 121-38.

[23] This theme is developed more extensively in Ivan Vallier, "Religious Elites: Differentiations and Developments in Roman Catholicism," in *Elites in Latin America,* pp. 190-232.

ond, some member of one's immediate or extended family may be in the priesthood, or may serve as a full-time employee in the Church's educational, mass media, or welfare programs. On another level, people frequently participate in Catholic-linked ceremonies and festivities, whether the Mardi Gras in Rio or the local *fiesta* that accompanies the celebration of one's saint's day. On state occasions, the bishop and other Church dignitaries accompany the key speaker to the platform and sit with him. Prayers and homilies may be offered. Throughout the hours of the day, Church bells mark the time, and special chimes toll important events or messages.

SUMMARY STATEMENT

The historical development of the Latin American continent is permeated with the presence of the Catholic Church, its traditions, values, and dogmas. Many of these cultural elements have lost their formal Catholic identity and have become fused with the general value system of nations. Under certain conditions, however, these latent, semiconscious, and religiously toned sentiments can be activated and channeled into Church support. There are only broad suggestions about the nature of these conditions, but it appears that two of the more important ones are (1) a national political crisis when fundamental principles of stability have been unexpectedly and deeply broken, and (2) direct attacks on the Church that are aimed toward eradicating its right to claim moral truths, or destroying its religious equipment and sanctuaries. In either of these two situations, the Church is funded with a large reservoir of traditional loyalty which may be channeled, often with dramatic consequences, into Church power.

These traditional patterns of Church–society relations share certain properties. First, they emphasize and reflect patterns of structural fusion and territorial or physical visibility. Diffuse control, rather than specialized, problem-solving structures, is the dominant mode. Second, these traditional bases of potential influence rely heavily on either top-level formal guarantees of privilege or informal personal networks tied to concrete and local units. The third pattern is reliance on general loyalties or religiously toned sentiments among the masses as a source of support. These principles set the stage, under conditions of threat and challenge, for coalitional arrangements with political groups, direct appeals to mass emotion, and direct hierarchical interventions into the public arena.

The traditional Church, in broad outlines, is a weak Church. It is weak because it tends to rely on external centers of sociopolitical power to maintain its semblance of a religious monopoly. This subjects it to the fluctuations and crises that characterize the political arena. It is also weak because the religio-Catholic loyalties that are stimulated by its beliefs and rituals are, first, found principally among sectors of the population who do not hold leadership positions in society (women, adolescents, rural folk) and, second, grounded on sentiments and expectations that are not mobilizable into continuous and consistent religious roles in the wider society. The most effective conditions for translating Catholic loyalties into organizational capital are crisis situations, i.e., when the "Church" or the "Catholic faith" is being directly attacked or threatened by enemies. This means that the Church gains its greatest strength in situations where it is required to rely on mass fear to defend itself. This defense, of course, reinforces traditional values, conservative extremism, and irrational leadership styles.

As a hypothesis, this suggests that the conservative nature of the Church is not a function of its formal doctrines and theological systems but stems from its features as a religious organization. These features—a scattered, segmental pattern of organization, weak

CHAPTER THREE

Catholicism, Integration, and Political Instability: A Hypothesis

administrative arrangements, low integration of religious expressions into its formal rituals—stimulate a symbiotic dependency on the wider system of traditional structures, old elites, and popular sentiments. The Church, viewed from these angles, has no autonomous religious charisma, no capacity to translate its "reserves of loyalty" into adaptive programs, and little, if any, internal integration that would help its officials to promote a steady, united front against social evils. Consequently it is a Church that can only react in terms of immediate pressures, which often means a turn to wider conservative forces. This very act provides those forces with needed symbolic meaning and indirect legitimation.

I shall take these ideas as a starting point for analyzing the problem of political instability in Latin America. My argument, briefly, is that the historical configurations that evolved in the relations between the Church and civil society obstructed the Church's potential capacities to create and institutionalize a religio-moral basis for social and political integration.[1] One of the byproducts is weak value consensus. In turn, the continuous turmoil that marks Latin American politics is consequence and symptom of this wider problem of value fragmentation. Social and political competition take place without the elastic backing of a religio-moral framework. Each struggle assumes the characteristics of an all-out battle over ultimate ends, rather than being a limited context whose participants share some "higher consensus" about the nature of society and its long-range purposes.

The Problem: Political Instability

The problem of political development in Latin America automatically draws attention to a series of patterns indicative of instability and crisis, e.g., protest movements, coups and rebellions, military interventions, weak coalitions among parties and interest groups, and rural violence. Specialists in Latin American political life have sought in numerous ways

[1] This thesis pushes the roots of the problem of social and political instability back into the early colonial period, rather than making the disruptions that characterized the independence period (1810-1830) the key. It also focuses attention on the institutional weaknesses of the colonial Church, instead of assuming that the Church was a forceful, superordinate, and primary integrative force. I suggest that the basic values and norms of Catholicism did not gain a major place in the definition of status relations and the central apparatus of social control, thus robbing the religious elites of a potential capacity to provide an autonomous, extrapolitical basis of cultural leverage. For another view on the historical relationship of Catholicism, culture, and the polity, see Richard M. Morse, "The Heritage of Latin America," in *The Founding of New Societies*, ed. Louis Hartz, *et. al.* (New York: Harcourt, Brace & World, Inc., 1964), esp. pp. 138-59.

to clarify and explain these recurring tendencies.[2] One of the most suggestive interpretations has been made by Kling, who sees political instability as correlated with foreign involvement in the domestic economies of Latin America, a conservative, landed elite, and the types of political competition that accompany these patterns.[3] Three general propositions are adduced by Kling:

1. High-level political offices in Latin American societies, by virtue of their linkages with foreign economic interests, are key opportunity bases for accumulating rapid, personal fortunes; i.e., political office can be exploited to draw down a share of foreign business profits or special fees.

2. Within these societies, the usual channels of economic mobility are blocked and monopolized by traditional economic groups, such as the landowners, thus rendering the forementioned political positions extremely significant as potential avenues for acquiring wealth.

3. The combination of blocked channels of economic mobility in the economic sector and the get-rich possibilities that are associated with certain types of political office provoke an atmosphere of social frustration and utopian ambitions that incites revolutions, coups, and political violence. In Kling's words:

As political office provides a uniquely dynamic opportunity to acquire an economic base of power, . . . sufficiently large segments of the population are prepared to take the ultimate risk, the risk of life, in a revolt, in a *coup d'état,* to perpetuate a characteristic feature of Latin American politics— chronic political instability. In the distinctive power structure of Latin America, government serves as a special transformer through which pass the currents of economic ambition.[4]

According to Kling, political instability is built into the colonial-type economic system, one in which the interests of outside business elites provide government officials with lucrative rewards so that the process of exploiting the Latin American economies can be continued. Although Kling does not proceed to formulate this theory into propositions amenable to comparative test, his analysis implies that political instability will vary positively with the strength of foreign economic interests in the national economies. He also implies that political instability will decrease as foreign capitalistic, exploitative interests are reduced.

Exploitation by foreign business interests, in combination with the

[2] For a summary of the main works and a presentation of a quantitatively-based argument of comparative scope, see D. P. Bwy, "Political Instability in Latin America: The Cross-Cultural Test of a Causal Model," *Latin American Research Review*, III, No. 2, 1968, 17-66.

[3] Merle Kling, "Toward a Theory of Power and Political Instability in Latin America," *The Western Political Quarterly*, IX, No. 1, March, 1956, 21-35.

[4] *Ibid.*, p. 33.

power of the traditional landowners, blocked mobility channels, and economic frustration, are important for understanding Latin America's chronic political instability. But it is misleading, in my judgment, to limit attention to these factors. Other lines of explanation deserve to be pursued. In the present instance, attention is placed on the relations between religion, the moral integration of society, and political action.[5] The main assumption is this: Political development in complex, changing societies requires the presence of an underlying core of religio-moral norms, which need to be relatively differentiated from the routine give and take of politics, so that a stable, yet flexible, framework of meanings, orientations, conceptions of the good society, and certain shared notions of human priorities is provided. This can be put into a broad hypothesis: Political instability in Latin America is bred, in part, by the absence of a durable religio-moral foundation within which political processes can be stabilized. Such basic integrative principles as cooperation, compromise, and mutual trust, which make up the cultural bases of institutional life, are weak. Consequently, political conflicts, short-run contests, and changes in political leadership are only tenuously linked with collective meanings about social goals and national objectives.

From this perspective, the crux of the political problem is not to be discovered in the structure of government nor in the personalities of the leaders and officials, but in the relation between the cultural sphere and the polity as a key subsystem of the society. The crucial intervening variable is the nature of the moral consensus that grounds the political process. The generation, consolidation, and allocation of political power depends on the prior presence and general strength of a moral-integrative framework that legitimates power and provides consensual norms for its operation—a framework that exists differentiated from the immediate political arena, routine disputes, and conflicts that are normal, expected corollaries of political life. The "political" process—short-run power-oriented contests—cannot become an effective mechanism if each political

---

[5] Although the role of religious beliefs and sentiments in the development of the moral-integrative bases of social life has received explicit attention from the time of Émile Durkheim, these relationships are usually assumed to exist, rather than being taken as foci of study in terms of how they develop or the factors that block their institutionalization. Even less attention has been given to the ways in which the absence or weakness of moral-integrative factors affects the political sphere. It is one thing to establish that moral-integrative factors play a key role in social life; it is quite another problem to ascertain the conditions under which these factors gain an institutionalized status or, conversely, the conditions that interrupt, weaken, or destroy them. For a full and unparalleled analysis of Durkheim's contributions to our understanding of the role of moral elements in social action, see Talcott Parsons, *The Structure of Social Action* (New York: McGraw-Hill Book Company, 1937), pp. 308-470.

encounter among the claimants triggers a "death struggle" over ultimate ends and basic values. Of course, these values have to be constantly appraised, revised, and criticized as part of a nation's evolutionary change. However, if these phenomena become enmeshed in the normal political encounters, the possibilities for formulating long-range objectives and initiating collective action are cut short. Since basic values, rather than policies and procedures, assume a central position in the political arena, the entire structural basis of society is continually placed in turmoil.[6]

SOURCES OF THE CHURCH'S FAILURE TO PROVIDE
RELIGIO-MORAL AUTHORITY

A religion is unique among human institutions in its potential capacities for creating general frameworks of meaning and universal standards of socioethical behavior. By holding intimate ties with the supernatural, a religion possesses a kind of symbolic freedom that allows it to construct theodicies, systems of reward and punishment, and theories of legitimation that do not have to stand the test of empirical verification. For these reasons, religions can be either revolutionary forces or buttresses of an extreme conservatism. However, these potentialities are not realized automatically. If a religious system, as represented by its spokesmen and elites, becomes identified with a particular political group and finds that its survival is bound up with the survival of that group, it loses an autonomous position of leverage to build and create a generalized system of meanings. Instead of functioning as a carrier and refurbisher of common values and social consensus, it becomes an ideology for a special interest group or a political power structure. Instead of the religion providing a higher order of meanings and value standards, it drops into an identifiable position in the stratification system. Its activities and pronouncements are viewed by the nonprivileged groups as part of the dominant power system. If this happens, the distinction between the political and

6 For Anderson, the distinctive feature of the Latin American political system is "tentativeness," i.e., a recurring pattern of intermittent balances that results from short-term coalitions and reciprocities among major power contenders. These fluctuations reflect (1) competing conceptions of legitimacy and the political process, (2) a continuing effort of rising power groups to gain admittance into the political arena, and (3) a persistence, rather than an elimination, of traditional power groups. The so-called revolutions in history are not considered revolutionary by Anderson because they failed to eliminate traditional power groups and traditional means of mobilizing power. Mexico, Bolivia, and Cuba are analyzed as exceptions. Anderson also holds that the Church remains a major power contender in the political sphere. Charles W. Anderson, "Toward a Theory of Latin American Politics," *Occasional Paper No. 2* (Nashville, Tenn.: Vanderbilt University, The Graduate Center for Latin American Studies, February, 1964), pp. 1-16.

religious spheres collapses. Competition and social conflict emerge as naked struggles of force and power, rather than as processes of give and take that can be muted and sustained by a set of common beliefs of a more general nature.

Although the historical record would require qualifications on many points, I suggest that a broad fusion between religious authority and political power occurred in Latin Ameria which, in turn, interrupted the potential capacities of the Church to author and sustain a general moral-integrative framework. Out of the interdependencies that grew up between the Crown, the civil authorities in the colonies, and the Church, several patterns of social control and structural development emerged: (1) a disregard for the detailed, formal regulations supplied by the Crown, since these did not always supply meaningful bases for resolving everyday problems of an administrative and political nature; (2) a social centrifugality accelerated by a proliferation of frontier settlements that possessed only weak and intermittent ties with the central cities; and (3) a system of special legal jurisdictions, as in the case of the Church, which possessed its own court system (fuero eclesiástico).

These configurations, along with many more specific tendencies, helped to weaken the linkages between law and "social order" and to separate the religious authority of the Church from the legal basis of society. It appears that this situation approximated Parsons' description of systems in which a tendency exists "to treat 'justice' as a direct implementation of precepts of religious and moral conduct . . . without institutionalizing an independent system of *societal* norms, adapted to the function of social control at the societal level and integrated on its own terms." [7] There were, however, two more specific patterns in the relation of the Church to society and in the propagation of its own work that deserve mention, both of which I consider important for understanding the Church's low capacity to generate an independent basis for helping to create and legitimize societal norms.

Civil control over the clergy and the functioning of the Church. [8] Dur-

[7] Talcott Parsons, "Evolutionary Universals in Society," *American Sociological Review*, XXIX, No. 3, June, 1964, 352. Italics in original.

[8] The main issue, with respect to the relation of the Church to the Crown and its political representatives, was the clergy's general lack of decision-making autonomy in relation to initiating new missionary work, adding new clergy, establishing dioceses, appointing bishops, and developing educational and eleemosynary institutions. Although these controls were balanced out to a large extent by the Crown's extension of special benefits to the Church (e.g., financial support, the granting to the clergy of exemptions from civil courts, and the defense of the Church against religious competitors and atheists), the fact remains that the Church, *qua* religious system, did not possess a differential status in society. Consequently, it did not possess a basis for developing an ethical evaluation of society, nor did it

ing the colonial period, the Church and the "State" were not co-partners. Instead, the relationship was hierarchical, with the Church holding the lower position. Civil control, legitimated by negotiations between the popes and the Catholic sovereigns of Spain (1485–1510), extended over every major sphere of Church activity: nominations to ecclesiastical offices, missionary work, finances, intra-Church communications, privileges of the clergy, and educational policies. Catholicism developed as a "kept Church," thus initiating patterns of ecclesiastical dependency and political involvement. These patterns are still prominently visible in many Latin American countries.

In this situation of subordination, Church elites were forced to play politics and to attempt gains for their own interests within short-term limits. Consequently, the potential capacity of the clergy to articulate a set of extrapolitical religious values and a system of meaningful, universal moral standards was drastically reduced. Instead of developing as agents of religious universals and sociomoral principles, the Church leaders became permanent auxiliary fixtures within the civil apparatus of power. Put another way, the subordination of the Church to the civil power structure prevented the clergy, with some exceptions, from locating an outside point of leverage from which general moral rules and standards of supernatural order could be formulated and institutionalized.

In that situation, the Church elites were unable to set long-range spiritual objectives, they could not develop a common basis for strengthening spiritual authority, they were unable to evaluate political policies on the basis of an articulated Christian position, and they were incapable of removing themselves from the daily political and administrative contests that emerged in an extensive overseas empire. These historical conditions served, in part, to tie the symbols of religious authority to both political maneuvering and a disrespect for moral rules.[9] When "the highest agents of God" take sides, disagree among themselves, bend to civil power, and violate their own religious teachings, what happens to the development of the religio-cultural matrix on which value consensus depends? The broad effect is that the possibility for creating a basis for

---

have to meet competition from other organized religious groups. The Church gained a monopoly on the basis of political protection, not from its capacities as a charismatic and innovative religious enterprise. For details on the origins and evolution of the relationship between the Crown and the Church, see J. Lloyd Mecham, *Church and State in Latin America: A History of Politico-Ecclesiastical Relations,* rev. ed. (Chapel Hill: University of North Carolina Press, 1966), pp. 3-37.

9 The fact that the Inquisition was completely under the control of the King—he appointed the inquisitors and they were solely responsible to him—indicates that the Church, as a formal organization, was encapsulated in and subordinate to the civil-political elites. See Mecham, *Church and State in Latin America,* pp. 34-35.

social consensus is ruptured; an overarching sense of moral meaning is absent; the political process becomes tied to immediate issues in such a way that each dispute and each conflict challenges the legitimacy of the whole system. Consequently, no appeal can be made to broad, shared values because these are weak and undeveloped. Meaning, under the circumstances, has to be generated by recourse to dramatic ideological concepts or a turn to military force.

Since no one in the system can predict the outcome of political processes, each interest group works out informal protective guarantees instead of investing commitments in activities related to the collective welfare. This pattern of weak social integration that underlies chronic instability cannot be explained by limiting attention to national temperament or to foreign exploitation. It must be located in the cultural foundations of the social order; more particularly in those groups and institutions which held the major potential for creating, developing, and institutionalizing a basis of moral solidarity. In Latin America, these considerations lead immediately to the Roman Catholic Church, its historical relations with centers of secular control, and its pastoral emphases.

The Church never completed its missionary task. The whole rationale for the conquest of the Americas was to take Christianity, i.e., the Holy Catholic Church, to pagan peoples. Civil, military, and ecclesiastical resources were initially organized with this goal in mind. A missionary zeal infiltrated the entire spectrum of colonizing ventures during the sixteenth century. Priests and friars, as specialists in this missionary cause, exhibited extraordinary qualities of courage, patience, and obedience in the earliest phase of this Christian campaign.

By the middle of the seventeenth century, most of the natives had been subdued. The fervor of colonization was depleted. Diocesan clergy, urban hierarchies, and the machinery of the Inquisition held the focal roles in ecclesiastical life.[10] Although missionary work continued in frontier zones and among settled tribes, the proselytizing posture of the Church was broken. With the consolidation of the empire and the growth of economic interests, the Church elites could assume that the Christianization process was complete. Thus they turned to the tasks of educating the children of the upper class, caring for the sick, and dispensing charity. Picón-Salas

---

[10] For a detailed descriptive history of the growth, extension, and consolidation of the Church in Latin America, see León Lopetegui and Félix Zubillaga, *Historia de la Iglesia en la América Española, Desde el Descubrimiento hasta Comienzos del Siglo XIX. México, América Central, Antillas* (Madrid: Biblioteca de Autores Cristanos, 1965); and Antonio de Egaña, *Historia de la Iglesia en la América Española, Desde el Descubrimiento hasta Comienzos del Siglo XIX. Hemisferio Sur* (Madrid: Biblioteca de Autores Cristianos, 1966).

provides a telling description of the seventeenth century in Spanish America:

> As the sixteenth century merged into the seventeenth, the Church likewise grew more sedentary and fond of luxury. It was more interested in dominating the Creole society of Spanish Americans than in harvesting Indian souls. . . . Immense wealth became unproductive as it flowed into the coffers of the religious orders and of the dioceses from the tithes and first fruits, from contributions of the crown and of feudal overlords. . . . The church-fortress, or evangelistic training center, of the early missionaries evolved into the elaborately ornate baroque structures of Spanish Creole architecture, and most of the intrigues in colonial cities emanated from the locutories of sumptuous convents.[11]

The bearing of the Church's shift in outlook and emphasis for the problems of political instability is twofold: First, the relaxation of missionary activity interrupted the growth of a strong religiously based relationship between the clergy and the people. A missionary emphasis implies outreach—going to the people, making contact with them, teaching the faith, and persuading them to join a religious fellowship. Religious principles are the primary basis of exchange and communication. In a second way, the reduction of missionary concern indicates that the Church leaders measured the growth of Christianization by the growth of the empire as a political and economic system. Colonization equaled Christianization. For this reason, the Church did not have to be preoccupied about the strength of its religious life at the grass roots. Unwittingly, this lack of concern for strong religious motivations locked the Church into a position of extreme dependency on the secular order. So long as the political situation remained viable and supportive of the formal Church, the territory was considered to be Christian. But in periods of crisis or conflict, the Church was unable to stand on its own as a general source of moral authority or as a carrier of basic values capable of encompassing, yet standing above parties in the dispute.

By giving up the missionary thrust (and with it the possibilities of building up a strong religiously based relationship with the people and the capacity to achieve autonomous religious strength outside the comforting embrace of the political order), the Church lost one of its key opportunities to form and create a culturally based system of religio-ethical leadership. In one sense, it missed the chance to undergo a process of differentiation from the short-term, conflict-focused political sector.

[11] Mariano Picón-Salas, *A Cultural History of Spanish America*, trans. Irving A. Leonard (originally published in Mexico, 1944), (Berkeley and Los Angeles: University of California Press, 1963), pp. 74, 75.

This is one of the main reasons for the characteristic contemporary Latin American political pattern of abrupt swings, radical breaks, and internal fragmentation: The underlying religio-moral basis of general values is absent. There is no stable extrapolitical framework within which political alternatives and lines of coalition can be related.

The seeds of this pattern were sown in the original relation between the colonial administration and the Church, but it received further cultivation by the Church leaders' mistaken assumption that political control in a territory implied Christian solidity. The basic elements of these developments may be clarified by a schematic diagram.

Two principles are displayed in Figure 3.1: (1) The political order in the colonial period mothered the Church, encapsulating it and using it as an auxiliary mechanism of secular control. Lacking autonomy, the Church had no point of external leverage on which it could build a broader system of norms, priorities, and higher level value principles. (2) Once this order was broken, and the political sphere emerged as a series of move-

FIGURE 3.1

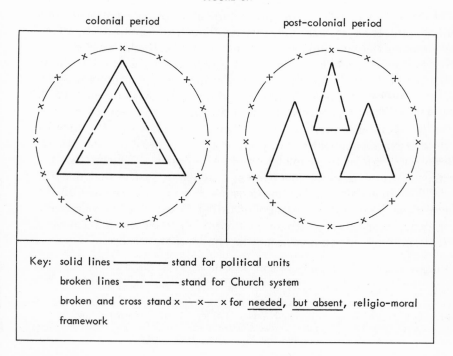

colonial period   post-colonial period

Key: solid lines ——————— stand for political units

broken lines —— —— —— stand for Church system

broken and cross stand x ——x—— x for needed, but absent, religio-moral

framework

ments and pressure groups, the Church lost its traditional support—stimulating its inherent political tendencies. Correspondingly, the "parties" to the political contest began to battle one another without the stabilizing backdrop of common values or "ultimate truths." The political process was turned loose in a situation where only utopian promises, armed force, or personal charisma could swing loyalties. But each of these mechanisms is a short-run device; none possesses "carrying power," nor is any an extension of a wider political culture that is grounded in the value system. Consequently, each political event or political contest has to create its own direction of order and, once created, the political group that wins is obligated to expend most of its energies on shoring up the fragile balance that has been gained instead of applying its resources toward the achievement of collective goals. When the Argentine writer Murena defines the nation's crisis as "the lack of community" and adds that "we do not form a body, though we may form a conglomeration," he has expressed the theme of the present theory, though he does not pursue the problem of explanation. His only question, "Who is to blame?" is answered elliptically: "No one. Everyone." [12]

From this perspective, the chronic intervention of the military takes on new meaning. Organized force, "in the interests of the people," becomes a temporary, intermittent substitute for a broader moral consensus that does not exist. The military bring a combination of naked strength and "moral" protection to bear on various "hopeless" political situations. Many people view the military as agents of national values, yet if these values had validity and held commitments of a broader nature than those required in politics, the military would not have the opportunity to intervene. There would be no necessity for sporadic take-overs by the "guardians of the values." The very fact that armed force is needed to inject one type of stability into the political process implies that the broader cultural bases of political stability are either very weak or nonexistent. We do not consider it completely beside the point to suggest that the military in Latin America functions as a religious system and that the Church, frequently enough, functions as a political system.[13] If the Church had developed as a symbol of extrapolitical religious values and as an extrapolitical agency of moral authority, the tacit encouragement of periodic military intervention would be considerably weaker.

[12] H. A. Murena, "Notas sobre le crisis argentina," *SUR*, No. 248, Buenos Aires, 1957; reprinted in *South America*, ed. Lewis Hanke (Princeton, N.J.: D. Van Nostrand Co., Inc., Anvil Book, 1959), p. 161.

[13] For a more extended discussion of this point in relation to the institutions of Latin America, see Ivan Vallier and Vivian Vallier, "South American Society," in *International Encyclopedia of the Social Sciences*, ed. David L. Sills, Vol. 15 (New York: The Macmillan Company and the Free Press, 1968), 64-77.

Two broad themes have been developed to provide an overview of the sociological setting of religio-moral authority in Latin America and the bearing of these patterns on the problem of political instability. The first theme stresses the close, but subordinate, involvement of the Church elites with secular matters with the consequence that the symbolic agents of ultimate values and moral authority fluctuated and wobbled with the play of local political events and power conflicts. The broad result was moral confusion. The people were unable to find a stable focus for legitimating key values. Church leaders, by virtue of their dependency and involvement, could not be trusted to take a consistent and meaningful stand on issues of general importance. Consequently, the basis for the development and institutionalization of a common, overarching religious-ethical framework never took shape. The special efforts of rebel priests, such as Las Casas,[14] to form this religious foundation were not successful, even though temporary gains were achieved.

The second theme we have stressed pertains to the interruption of the Church's missionary posture which, in effect, reduced its opportunities for creating a religiously based type of strength within the colonial setting. If the missionary task had received front-rank attention and pastoral work had developed accordingly, the Church would not have found itself without internal sources of strength when the practical order of the colonial period collapsed. Lacking this strength and without a clear sense of the religious task, the Church had to take sides with political groups as a means of survival. This drew the religious elites right back into the political arena and thus excluded their possibilities for achieving a broader, extrapolitical position. When a religious system discovers that its internal, spiritual life is decayed and unfocused, it turns to outside sources of support and protection.

Since the liberal movements in the nineteenth century defined the Church as the key enemy, the religious elites quickly became eager participants in the conservative cause. Had the Church stood "above politics," the liberals could have drawn legitimation from a broader value framework. There is little doubt that this kind of support would have given the Latin American liberal movement a solid basis on which to develop and grow. Lacking this kind of internal "religious" sponsorship, the liberal movement faltered, developed serious internal fissures, and in most respects failed to achieve institutionalization. By abandoning the Church, under conditions that seemed to require it, the liberals weakened their

[14] For a description of the role of Bartolomé de las Casas in the early development of the relations between religious norms of social justice and politico-economic exigencies, see Lopetegui and Zubillaga, *Historia de la Iglesia en la América Española,* pp. 106-17.

long-range possibilities. They soon learned that a liberal constitution, couched in winning paper phrases, is no substitute for a liberal movement that draws meaning and support from a "sacred" tradition.

Corollaries and Consequences

By placing the traditional Catholic system in the broader context of Latin America's problem of political order, a whole series of discrete patterns is clarified, providing an explanatory basis. From one side, the ideological content of Latin American life is placed in perspective. Ideologies are explicit systems of ideas and symbols that are intended to legitimate and give meaning to a set of political interests.[15] These ideologies may be derived from a wider system of values, or they may be aimed toward the establishment of a set of values. In both instances, ideology stands as a more concrete, focused, and lower level articulation of norms and ideas.

In the Latin American situation, ideology takes on a special kind of primacy in the political process because the expected and needed value orientations, at the higher level of culture, are not clearly formed; furthermore, they are not unified, and they do not serve as a focus for building social consensus. Consequently, each bid for power must be accompanied by a creation of a set of legitimating ideas in the hope that these prepared formulas will draw commitments, loyalties, and momentum.

In a very important sense, the flowering of ideologies indicates a low level of common values and a weak capacity of the political system to transform interests into an integrated program of national development. If the initial place of the Church had allowed for the extrapolitical growth of an overarching set of meaningful value orientations, flexible yet stable, the routine conflicts and cleavages that are inherent features of the political process could have functioned as an arena for deciding procedures and alternative policies, rather than becoming a battleground for defining and articulating values. This is not to say that the value systems are not legitimate concerns of political life. Rather, if value competition enters into every political encounter, all the energies are dissipated on building temporary commitments and victory-focused strategies, leaving the leaders, once in office, without a stable basis on which to bring the resource of power to bear on the attainment of collective goals.

In short, Roman Catholicism as a religious system holds the potential capacity to function as an agency of universal values and as one contribution to a system of social integration. Possessing a unique combination of

[15] A more general conception of ideology is provided by Clifford Geertz, "Ideology as a Cultural System," in *Ideology and Discontent,* ed. David E. Apter (New York: The Free Press of Glencoe, Inc., 1964), pp. 47-76.

a legal tradition derived from the Romans, a set of ethical principles drawn from the Christian faith, and an elaborate system of organized statuses geared to spiritual and pastoral functions, the Church carries the possibilities for developing a stable, religio-cultural framework. Yet it has not, for reasons already given. One of the unfortunate consequences is continually evidenced by the political turmoil in contemporary Latin America.

From another side, the whole problem of Church–State relations takes on new dimensions. The great bulk of scholarship that now exists on Church and State in Latin America is made up of concrete descriptions of this relation in a given time and place. From this, one gains a perspective on variations, special issues, and the features of formal contracts, such as the concordata, constitutional statutes, and the like. But a preoccupation with these patterns has stood in the way of more theoretical quesions, e.g., why does the "State" seem to need the support of the Church and vice-versa? What limited political functions does the Church perform and under what conditions? At what point in the development of national politics can the State afford to "let go" of the Church? This same question can be asked for the Church: What kinds of internal religious strengths are prerequisite for autonomous Church development? These and other questions quickly emerge from a perspective that gives first priority to the relations of cultural values, religious leadership, and the political process.

The concrete patterns that have developed and that now exist between Church and State in Latin American societies are, in part, expressions of the more fundamental problem of weak consensual values. Political leaders court the support of the Church or subordinate its functioning to the machinery of government because they realize that certain junctures in the political process cannot be passed without the help of the Church, either as a mechanism for forming public opinion or as a source of legitimation. The Church's capacity to mobilize public opinion on an issue, once it has come out into the open, has been demonstrated on numerous occasions. Equally important, the symbolic presence of the Church within the broader sphere of governmental activity frequently allows the political leader to provide his course of action with an added source of legitimation.

In this respect, Peronismo and the APRA movement provide interesting contrasts. The Apristas infused their ideology with strong moral principles and symbols, but they did not seek the support of the Church.[16] They championed the full separation of Church and State, as well as full

16 Harry Kantor, *The Ideology and Program of the Peruvian Aprista Movement*, 2nd ed. (Washington, D.C.: Saville Books, 1966), pp. 60-65.

religious freedom for the individual. For a number of reasons, the Apristas never got off the ground. If the present line of analysis is valid, one of the factors in the Aprista failure pattern is their mistaken assumption that a popular movement could develop and achieve political power without the legitimating support of the Church. By contrast, Perón made rapid moves to bring the Church to his side. While the two systems worked together, Peronismo succeeded. But once Perón overstepped the boundaries and tried to legislate in areas of social life that are of deep concern to the Church, his leadership and his movement fell.[17]

IMPLICATIONS OF THE HYPOTHESIS

Traditional Catholicism in Latin America is usually discussed in terms of supernatural outlooks, ritual practices, and indigenous cults. These are justifiable topics within a descriptive profile. Yet an emphasis on these configurations tends to deflect attention from a whole range of underlying sociological issues, such as the religious tradition's relation to culture, the ways in which moral and legal norms are connected, and the political implications of a pastorally weak Church. These issues point to the *relational* implications of a religion's features, operating styles, and mechanisms of control or influence. Few religions can be understood, much less integrated into sociological theories, if they are viewed as things in themselves or approached in terms of individuals' orientations and practices. The relational or systemic aspects are always to be considered, even if this means employing tentative heuristic concepts and excluding certain historical details.

In the foregoing sections of this chapter, an attempt has been made to place the operating characteristics of the historical Church into the wider pattern of weak value consensus and its corollaries: low societal integration and political instability. This hypothesis does not purport to state a single-cause explanation for all instances of political instability in Latin American societies, nor does it exclude other hypotheses that may point to connections between traditional Catholicism and economic variables. Its main purpose has been to call attention to the role of general, and religiously grounded, values in the development of a social order and how, in turn, political processes are implicated therein. This does not mean that there is equivalence between the existence of a social order and social conservatism. Quite the contrary. It only suggests that the processes of political change and modernization, more generally, can be

[17] For a description of the events that led to the break between Perón and the Church, see Robert J. Alexander, *The Perón Era* (New York: Columbia University Press, 1951), pp. 125 ff.

continuously interrupted, if not paralyzed, in situations where a generalized basis of moral integration is absent.

The hypothesis I have presented assumes that this basic integration is
extremely weak in many Latin American contexts and that this weakness
is, in part, a product of the Church's historical incapacities to formulate,
articulate, and sustain a position as an agency of religious values. By
becoming encapsulated in a system of control mechanisms that made
survival dependent on political arrangements, it could neither promote
an ethically based criticism of social institutions nor generate a religious
charisma that would bind members into a spiritual community. These
patterns are not unique, except in details, to Latin America. Other religious systems, including Eastern Orthodoxy and, to some degree, Roman
Catholicism in Spain, Portugal, and Italy, share some of the same institutional disabilities. The French case is quite different, as is the case of the
United States. In both these situations, the Church was forced to meet
major forms of value competition (not just political opposition) before
the beginning of the nineteenth century. In turn, both Church systems
have developed adaptive styles that allow them to hold certain integral
ties with the total culture, concurrently fostering a series of nonpolitical
ties with the wider society.

How a religious system develops its mechanisms of control and influence becomes a problem of general significance for social change and
social stability. If it abandons a direct reliance on political groups, it may
forfeit some of its short-term security but, concurrently, gain possibilities
for linking itself to the total cultural system and for generating religious
charisma. If these shifts occur, a whole range of new bases of influence
are opened which do not impinge directly on the political arena. In
short, it becomes differentiated from secular power arrangements while
taking on a fusion with the wider system of values, cultural symbols, and
general beliefs.

In the remaining chapters of the book, attention is directed toward the
lines of change, differentiation, and development that are occurring in
Latin American Catholicism. Some of these carry significant implications
for the restructuring of Catholic influence. Others tend to be novel extensions of traditional principles. How they are being combined and
related to the institutional Church indicates something about the whole
process, and possibility, of Catholic development.

Traditional configurations continue to dominate Latin American Catholicism. Religious motivations and beliefs remain heavily tied to other-worldly values and quasi-magical frameworks. Most officials of the Church, in turn, continue to rely on political connections and legal statutes to guarantee the dominance of their institution. In the local parishes, the majority of the clergy still lack integral relationships with the members. Extrasacramental forms of devotion and worship continue to be the basic modes of spiritual activity. Yet the balance between these traditional tendencies and progressive forces in the Church is shifting.

The groups and movements that make up the growing progressive sector are diverse in terms of stated objectives and theological rationale, and in their relations with the hierarchy. Differing aspects of social life and political reality are selected as foci of potential influence. Specialized educational programs, fusing literacy training with political concepts, compete with social service programs and the development of ecumenical relations. Within the internal life of the Church, ideas and themes emanating from the Second Vatican Council (1962-1965) compete with more radical conceptions of worship, association, and secular action. In recent years many reports and commentaries on these diverse initiatives have been

CHAPTER FOUR

Changing Strategies of Church Influence: Evolutionary Principles

published,[1] but little is being done to relate them to one another, or to identify the roles they play in the wider process of restructuring influence.[2]

This chapter is an attempt to distinguish the underlying features of these newer developments and to assess their significance for the Church's changing relation to society. Four sections divide the chapter. Section one describes the new pressures and competitive forces that threaten the traditional Church. The second section identifies the basic strategies of influence that have emerged over the past half century and that now compete for ascendancy within the progressive sector of the Church.. In section three, these recent strategies, in combination with two traditional ones, are examined as part of a general evolutionary model of Church influence. The final section discusses the responses of Churches that stand at differing stages of development to outside threats and challenges.

THREATS AND PRESSURES: THREE LEVELS [3]

The traditional Church, especially during the past fifty years, has in one Latin American country after another encountered trends and events that are forcing its elites to recognize a state of bankruptcy. The credits of the Church, built up over the years through political coalitions, a permissive morality, property involvements, and other worldly promises, are largely depleted. This crisis is partly due to the anticlerical attacks of the

[1] The most complete information on the "new forces" in Latin American Catholicism over the past ten years is available in the Center for Intercultural Formation Reports (CIF Reports) and Intercultural Center of Documentation (CIDOC) materials distributed by the Center developed by Ivan Illich in Cuernavaca, Mexico. The CIF Reports, containing original articles and descriptive information on changes in the Church, were published from 1962 to 1967. The CIDOC documents, distributed from 1967, are reproductions of essays, articles, and conference reports pertaining to the ideology, institutions, and programs of the progressive and radical groups in the Church. The Center for Intercultural Formation also publishes a series of monographs, entitled "Soundings" (SONDEOS), on religious phenomena in Latin America.

[2] An exceptionally fine set of sociological essays on change and modernization in Latin American Catholicism has been written by Thomas G. Sanders during 1967 and 1968 as field reports to the Institute of Current World Affairs, 366 Madison Ave., New York, N.Y. The topics covered in these reports include: "Two Catholic Innovating Elites," "CELAM (The Latin American Bishops' Council)," "The Evolution of a Catholic Intellectual," "Family Planning in Chile," "A Typology of Catholic Elites," and "The Priests of the People." Dr. Sanders is presently the Latin American field representative for the American Universities Field Staff, Inc., 366 Madison Ave., New York, N.Y.

[3] This section is a slightly revised version of part of the previously published essay, Ivan Vallier, "Religious Elites: Differentiations and Developments in Roman Catholicism," in Elites in Latin America, eds. Seymour Martin Lipset and Aldo Solari (New York: Oxford University Press, Inc., 1967), pp. 190-232. Permission granted from publisher.

nineteenth century that forced the Church out of key areas of public life; more important, however, is a series of subtle sociological trends that have more recently cut across the whole social order: the growth of an urban-based working class, population shifts, a strengthening of technical and scientific centers in secular universities, and the emergence of aggressive interest groups, which make clamorous and immediate demands on the resources of these societies. Old and familiar lines of power, influence, and status are weakened and confused, if not totally broken.

Out of these general changes, brought on by both the evolution of Western civilization and by indigenous strivings, three developments have appeared to render traditional Catholicism's position of influence especially problematic: new value movements, a changed basis of social control and group integration in society, and certain pressures of non-Latin American Catholic hierarchies on the leaders and laity of the national churches. Each of these threats deserves separate comment.

Local—New value movements. Up until the turn of the century, Catholicism held a dual monopoly. It stood, on the one hand, as the official national religion of these republics (and in some cases, still does). In addition, Catholicism held an undisputed dominance as a general religious culture. Most of the value orientations, cognitive frameworks, and notions of rightness were part and parcel of the Catholic religious framework. Even anticlerical intellectuals of the nineteenth century willingly evidenced deep respect and feeling for this overarching religious phenomenon.

Two kinds of radical movements, both arising within the past half century, have helped to break this cultural monopoly of Catholicism: political movements of the left [4] and salvation-oriented Protestant sects.[5] Both movements preach a new reward system, assume a militant posture against the existing social order, and articulate a cohesive set of anti-Catholic values. The rapid growth of these movements between the first World War and 1950 severed the Latin American value system, at least in some countries, from the Catholic religious system. Chile, of course, stands out in this respect. Mexico, somewhat a special case, went through the same process, although with violence and abruptness. Brazil would appear to be almost as far along in terms of this split as Chile. But the

[4] Robert J. Alexander, *Communism in Latin America* (New Brunswick, N.J.: Rutgers University Press, 1957); William Pierson and Frederico G. Gil, *Governments of Latin America* (New York: McGraw-Hill Book Company, 1957); and Kalman H. Silvert, *The Conflict Society* (New Orleans: Hauser Press, 1961).

[5] Kenneth Strachan, *The Missionary Movement of the Non-Historical Groups in Latin America* (New York: Division of Foreign Missions of the National Council of Churches of Christ in the U.S.A., 1957); Prudencio Damboriena, "The Pentecostals in Chile," *Catholic Mind,* LX (1962), 27-32.

important thing is that, for the first time, a line was cut between a value system fused with Catholicism and a non-Catholic value system. Where the earlier anticlerical movement had forced the Church, as an organization, out of certain public spheres, these new value movements forced the religion to take a competitive position at the level of major values. In one sense, Catholicism was pushed down one level of social control, taking on the color of an ideology for the conservative groups. One outcome of this shift was the placing of the Church in a position where its fortunes rested with a limited segment of society and one which, in terms of rapidly growing social trends, was on the decline.

But the competition at the level of values turned out to be only one of the threats posed by these new value movements. Besides offering a whole new framework of "salvation," new meanings, and new categories of evaluation, they also provided the adherents with a "program" and a "strategy of action" in society. Moreover, both the Communist-Socialist movement and the Pentecostals sponsored a lay ethic that provided both new and old members with roles that allowed full participation. Value commitments could be linked to group responsibility.[6] Consequently, the Catholic Church found itself in competition with morally oriented action systems that were linked with society at the grass roots (among groups that the Church had not integrated), and that provided the membership with "opportunity structures" which, in most instances, served as effective bridging mechanisms between commitment and organizational participation. The layman, even the novice, found himself with a definite status, a set of meaningful activities, and with delegated responsibility, e.g., contacting potential members, "selling the gospel," and so on.

The traditional Catholic system, as I've tried to indicate earlier, is ill-equipped to counter these militant, focused, sect-type value movements. For more than four centuries, the "ordinary member" was overlooked as a religious system resource. No attempts were made by the hierarchy to integrate the layman into the religious organization, or to provide him with a set of meaningful responsibilities. This is not surprising. Legal and logical reasons (having to do with the *official* status of the layman) aside, the traditional Catholic system in Latin America has not had to groom the layman as an instrument of religious influence or anchorage since, in fact, the whole Catholic system was sponsored, protected, supported, and cradled by the total society, especially the

---

[6] Lipset underlines the decided parallels between religious sects and Communist movements, particularly in terms of the status groups which respond. This is shown on the basis of comparative data for America and Western Europe. S. M. Lipset, "Extremism, Political and Religious," in *Political Man*, ed. S. M. Lipset (Garden City, N.Y.: Doubleday & Company, Inc., 1960), pp. 107-8.

conservative political system. Why, then, should the grass roots, or the laity, be shaped, organized, and delegated to "win the neighbor"? All the neighbors were baptized Catholics, so were the people of the next village, so too were patrons and slaves, peasants, and military officers. In short, building up and channeling a membership-based religious enthusiasm were not essential to the operation and viability of the traditional Catholic system.

One further characteristic of the new value movements deserves attention, for again it is something that the traditional Catholic system is unable to offer. I have in mind the emphasis placed in these new value movements on strong person-to-person bonds or "horizontal solidarity," caught up in such phrases as "From each according to his ability; to each according to his needs," and "We are all brothers in Christ: no priests, no servants, no rich, no poor." The Communists and Socialists, as well as the Pentecostals, stress these dimensions both ideologically and structurally. Contrast this with the traditional conceptions of status in the Catholic organization: priest above people, bishop above priest, and pope above all. Even within the laity, the social lines of division (class, family, ethnic, etc.) were allowed to hold their distinct visibility. Those who worshiped regularly within the same church building did not constitute a solidarity-based congregation, but a random assortment of differential social statuses juxtaposed in proximity for the duration of the mass. Traditional Catholicism does not provide the membership with religious conceptions that link men to other men in a form of familiar solidarity. For this type of gratification, the Catholic had to turn to devotional cults, family, friends, co-villagers, and extended kin. It is not surprising then to find that in Latin America these basic types of social relationships are resistant to change and modification.

National—The emergence of a new rhythm to society and its challenge to traditional religious control. The second major stimulus that increasingly pushes the Church toward self-evaluation, new strategies, and differing alignments with the secular world, is less easily defined and conceptualized than in the case of the earlier mentioned value movements. But it is no less significant. For want of a better term, I shall refer to this second stimulant as the aggregate effects of a modern society's rhythm—that is, there is a characteristic tendency for a modern, nationally focused society to move and adapt as a total system. As the Latin American countries develop economically and politically, a qualitatively different type of institutional interdependence emerges, binding all specialized functional units into a more functionally integrated whole. Thus, the *primary* integrative level of an industrializing country is found at the level of the total society, not in terms of regional or local (community, family, ethnic) units. This broad and often loose form of national integration characteristically generates its own peculiar dynamic expressed variously through geographical and social mobility, through the interplay of organized group interests, and in the continual adjustment of old norms against new emphases that emerge in the wake of innovation, structural change, and population shifts. National events dominate the rhythm of social life and are quickly transmitted, with varying repercussions, to all levels of human activity. This means that special interests, such as influence-oriented religious groups, require clear-cut national strategies and forceful national organizations if they are to make an impact. Furthermore, behaviors in key institutional spheres are highly segregated, thereby decreasing the possibility of controlling and influencing people through a single type of public activity. Thus, in order for a Church to "get at the people," more is required than programs of limited, local dimensions; more is required than *ad hoc,* short-term coalitions and maneuverings. Similarly, a program that is developed to gain influence at one point in time or in one geographical area may have to be quickly modified and/or shifted in location and emphasis, simply because residential and social involvements constantly undergo change, often quite abruptly. The web of life is difficult to hold in focus, except at the national level, and even more difficult to control. Transiency, flux, and movement—even though patterned within a broad institutional setting—give the modern industrial society the mark of a ceaselessly flowing current.

Threats emerge from all sides: increased competition with secular public agencies in areas of human need, the loss of control lines or connections with strategic centers of social control, and a reduced visibility in the sphere of religious leadership. In all this there is a marked uncertainty about "religious needs," an ambivalence over the proper functions of the Church, a confusion over priorities, a search for new resources, and a deep frustration bred by a vision of possibility and a simultaneous realization of inadequacy.

These developments hold a number of basic implications for an ambitious religious system. Several organizational tasks become imperative. First, the religious impact has to be planned, developed, and aimed along lines that catch hold of the total society's trends, rhythms, and problems. Second, gains or attempted gains require action—conscious outreach and coordinated maneuvering. Loyalty must be generated, not simply gathered. Third, religious programs must meet at least two organizational criteria: steady, long-term directedness, and short-range, local flexibility.

Specialization and performance must be matched by central decision making and effective coordination.

Traditional Catholicism, accustomed to maintaining its position through *ad hoc* problem solving, local adaptations, and alignment with prominent status groups (now on the way out), possesses limited organizational capacity to deal with this new rhythm of social life, particularly with regard to achieving an effective competitive position in this radically changed web of social control. The Church is still, in many cases, given to passivity and informal maneuvering, and is susceptible to norms and pressures in numerous particular situations. It is thus extremely handicapped. From its long years of accumulated involvements with multiple, concrete aspects of traditional life, it now finds the task of gathering itself together for purposes of building a new offensive next to impossible.

International—Non-Latin American Catholic hierarchies. Before going on to describe some of the key adaptive developments in certain Catholic systems, I want to identify at least one further source of pressure, perhaps even better termed a threat. Unbeknown to some observers of contemporary Latin American Catholicism, the Church is being put under heavy pressure by the various hierarchies of international Catholicism. Astute Roman Catholic leaders, representing the entire spectrum from the papacy to various national episcopal conferences (in France, Belgium, Germany, Canada, and the United States), are evidencing a first-order concern over the Church's problems in Latin America. Pressures are thereby placed on Latin American prelates to put their house in order.[7]

There are several reasons for this outside interest. Latin America not only encompasses more than one-third of the Church's total baptized membership but, as well, appears to be particularly susceptible to political seductions of the communist variety. Equally important, Vatican II quite plainly focused around issues, policies, and innovations that bear directly on the problems that are found in traditional Latin American Catholicism. No one can overlook the connections between the current emphases on liturgical innovations, the principle of collegiality, theological reforms, or extra-Catholic ecumenicity, and the present crisis of the Church in lands south of the border. Since Latin America undoubtedly stands as one of the key "test sites" for contemporary Catholicism, and since Vatican II is considered the major instrument for

[7] My main referent, when referring to the Latin American Church in this context, is the more traditional and conservative sectors, which plainly make up the bulk of its institutional life. I recognize that for many progressive Latin American churchmen these outside pressures appear as both conservative and "colonialist." The growing radicalization of the progressive groups in the Brazilian Church during recent months has, for example, led to "certain pressures" from Rome that are aimed to slow down their momentum. The local response is expectedly negative.

"bringing the Church up to date," it follows that the test of the Council is to be found in what happens to Catholicism in Latin America.

Traditional Catholicism is, accordingly, under severe threat from at least three levels of social reality: (1) the grass-roots level, augmented by the rapid successes of the new value movements; (2) the national or societal level, prompted by the radical changes in the patterned relations between institutional spheres and concrete social units; and (3) the international level, taking the form of goadings, criticisms, and urgings by other sectors of the Catholic hierarchy.

COMPETING NEW STRATEGIES OF INFLUENCE AND ACTION

Three basic lines of development, or influence strategies, are examined briefly: (1) the missionary strategy, (2) the social development strategy, and (3) the congregational strategy. Each strategy assumes a central task, takes account of a certain sector of the situation, and incorporates particular ideologies and organizational formats. Anyone familiar with recent trends in the Church will realize that these strategies do not touch upon all the efforts and initiatives that are under way. I do not, for example, discuss the Christian Democratic parties.[8] Although they hold an indirect relationship, at least in the minds of most people, to the Church, they are not explicit extensions of its institutional life. Similarly, I do not take up the varieties of local and diocesan programs that are generated by specific situations and problems. For present purposes, the primary focus is the national Church systems and continental-wide movements, with particular attention to the diversity of new perspectives and their implications for Catholicism's changing relations with society and culture.

The Missionary Strategy

The goals of this strategy are at least twofold: to make clergy and members aware of the Church's loss of societal dominance, and to motivate them to help recapture lost loyalties. The theologies that dominate this strategy are evangelical and militant, stressing terms such as "mission," "spiritual conquest," and "decisions of faith." Society is viewed as a mission territory, even though the majority of its members still adhere to a vague Catholic tradition. The primary mode of religious action is apostolic engagement in the world, or the conscious creation of opportunities for exerting Christian influence on individuals and structures. The

[8] See Chapter Five.

chief organizational mechanism created by the Church to promote the apostolic actions of laymen is Catholic Action.[9]

Catholic Action is a general term designating organized groups of laymen, sponsored by local bishops, which are intended to generate a militant enthusiasm for extending the Church's spiritual influence in society. The origins of Catholic Action can be traced back, in a loose way, to the efforts of Italian and French laymen in the late nineteenth century.[10] But the formal beginnings occurred during the pontificate of Pius XI (1922-1939).[11] During the late 1920s and the 1930s, Church officials legitimated and gave impetus to two distinct models of Catholic Action. General Catholic Action (often referred to as the Italian model) features a fourfold organizational pattern: youth and adults, male and female. The other model, known as specialized Catholic Action, is organized by sex in terms of occupational and class divisions, e.g., the Young Christian Workers, Catholic Action of University Students, Catholic Action of the Workers, etc. Whereas general Catholic Action tends to be organized around local parishes, specialized Catholic Action is more often tied directly to the bishop. Both systems incorporate priests as chaplains or ecclesiastical supervisors.

The enthusiasm Pius XI showed for Catholic Action, and its official standing, led to its general adoption throughout the Church. Bishops, often with some reluctance, attempted to establish such programs, recognizing their potential for reaching the youth and augmenting the Church's confessional strength in local situations. The social encyclicals of Leo XIII and Pius XI, along with the theological works of Jacques Maritain, provided the basic documents for study and training. During the 1930s Catholic Action movements grew rapidly throughout Western

---

[9] The best single work on the nature of Catholic Action and its place in the total framework of the Church's contemporary adaptations is Yves M. J. Congar, *Lay People in the Church*, rev. ed., trans. Donald Attwater (Glen Rock, N.J.: The Newman Press, 1965), [originally published as *Jalons pour une Théologie du Laïcat*] (Paris: Les Editions du Cerf, 1953), esp. Chapter VIII, "The Laity and the Church's Apostolic Function," pp. 349-99.

[10] For historical details on the emergence and growth of Catholic Action in Western Europe, see Joseph N. Moody, *et. al.*, *Church and Society. Catholic and Political Thought and Movements 1789-1950* (New York: Arts Inc., 1953); Jan Grootaers, "The Roman Catholic Church" in *The Layman in Christian History*, eds. Stephen Charles Neill and Hans-Ruedi Weber (Philadelphia: The Westminster Press, 1963), pp. 298-336; and Gianfranco Poggi, *Catholic Action in Italy. The Sociology of a Sponsored Organization* (Stanford, Calif.: Stanford University Press, 1967), pp. 14-44.

[11] The formal principles of Catholic Action were defined by Pius XI (1922-1939) in his encyclical *Quadragesimo Anno*, May 15, 1931, and in the allocution of Pius XII, *De Quelle Consolation*, October 14, 1951.

Europe. In Latin America, some beginnings were realized in major cities.[12] Special strength emerged in Chile, largely due to the capable efforts of particular men, such as Father Hurtado.[13] Another vigorous movement grew up in Rio de Janeiro around the Centro Dom Vital.[14] The Catholic Action programs in most other places throughout Latin America made only hesitant starts. Since the 1950s special efforts have been made to organize rural youth. This shift is undoubtedly closely related to the growing importance of the peasants as a social and political group.

However, Catholic Action programs have not gained a deep, institutional foothold among the Church's membership, nor have they generated new attachments to the faith among those who stand outside the sacramental life. Their most significant products are to be discovered at the ideological and organizational levels. Catholic Action, and especially its university programs, generated a reform-oriented social Catholicism that has played a key role in the Christian Democratic political movements. It was decisive in Chile for turning a certain number of Catholic youth away from the coalition that the Church held with the Conservative party. Moreover, it stimulated laymen to see political action as their responsibility, rather than that of Church officials.

On the organizational side, Catholic Action helped to build ties between national and local centers in terms of functional interests, thus helping to overcome the local segmental configurations that typified the Church in most places. Catholic Action also brought home the fact that the average member could not be easily mobilized into a militant apostle. The idea of taking up engagement in society as a spiritual agent of the Church carried little, if any, meaning. Confusion also arose around the relation of spiritual action to political action. The failure of Catholic Action to mobilize an auxiliary labor force indicated to Church leaders that new levels of motivational commitment had to be gained antecedent to the formation of apostolic programs. It also suggested that strategies other than spiritual conquest were needed to reach the rising groups in society.

[12] Country-by-country descriptions, in varying degrees of comprehensiveness, are provided in Richard Pattee, ed., *El Catolicismo Contemporaneo en Hispano-América* (Buenos Aires: Edition Fides, 1951).

[13] The leadership and organizational emphases of Father Hurtado are dealt with at length by Alejandro Magnet, *El Padre Hurtado*, 3rd ed. (Santiago, Chile, Editorial del Pacífico, S.A. 1957).

[14] M. Ancilla O'Neill, *Tristão de Athayde and the Catholic Social Movement in Brazil* (Washington, D.C.: The Catholic University of America Press, 1939).

The Social Development Strategy

A noticeable shift occurred in the efforts of progressive Church groups following World War II, and especially in the late 1950s. Instead of promoting the formation of Catholic youth and trying to mobilize militant cadres of spiritual apostles, increased amounts of attention were given to creating social, technical, and economic programs that would have a direct appeal to marginal status groups, such as the peasants and the urban poor. Catholic Action was not abandoned but incorporated as a kind of organizational base on which new activities could be built.

The product of these new initiatives was a diverse range of organized programs: vocational training centers for rural youth,[15] cooperatives for the poor (credit, housing, production), literacy courses [16] (carried forward either through radio broadcasting systems or through parish-based classes), health clinics, and agrarian reform projects.[17] Although each line of specialization differs in factual conditions of origin, type of sponsorship, geographical focus, and organizational format, they share at least a twofold objective: (1) an improvement of the personal and social capacities of marginal peoples, and (2) an expansion of the Church's contacts with social groups with which it had only weak, perhaps nonexistent, connections. This phase stimulated a general mood of entrepreneurship and innovation among priests and lay readers. Every leader with progressive inclinations felt himself under obligation to create a

[15] One of the most developed programs for rural life is found in Chile. See Oscar Dominguez, *El Campesino Chileno y la Acción Católica Rural* (Fribourg, Switzerland: Oficina Internacional de Investigaciones Sociales de FERES, 1961). Chile's Institute of Rural Education, within which some of the Church's main rural programs are organized, is described and evaluated by William J. Platt, *et. al., Training and Educational Needs in Chile's Agricultural Development* (Stanford, Calif.: Stanford Research Institute, June, 1965), pp. 51-56.

[16] The Colombian Church's system of rural education, *Acción Cultural Popular* (ACPO), is carried out through radio schools, leadership training centers, and a variety of specialized publications. A brief description of the program is provided by Emanuel de Kadt, "Paternalism and Populism: Catholicism in Latin America," *Journal of Contemporary History,* II, No. 4, October, 1967, pp. 91-93. Similar programs have been initiated in Brazil, as reported by David Mutchler, "Roman Catholicism in Brazil," *Studies in Comparative International Development,* I, No. 8 (1965), pp. 107-8. The Basic Education Movement in Brazil, representing a more radical approach to social and political training, is analyzed within the context of a broad range of new developments in the Church by Thomas G. Sanders, "Catholicism and Development: The Catholic Left in Brazil," in *Churches and States: The Religious Institution and Modernization,* ed. Kalman H. Silvert (New York: American Universities Field Staff, Inc., 1967), pp. 95-98.

[17] The Church's land reform experiments in the diocese of Talca, Chile, are given extended treatment by William C. Thiesenhusen, *Chile's Experiments in Agrarian Reform,* Land Economics Monograph No. 1 (Madison, Wis.: The University of Wisconsin Press, 1966), Chapters 2, 3, 4, and 5.

program that would help to upgrade the social conditions of the forgotten classes and, at the same time, foster the influence of the Church in society. These efforts were not political in any direct sense, but combined socio-economic goals with spiritual or religious objectives. Of course, the indirect political aspects were there.

The complex relations that grew up between Catholic Action organizations, social improvement programs, and the national governments can be illustrated by the case of the Institute of Rural Education in Chile. This center for the training of rural youth in agricultural and mechanical skills emerged in 1955. However, its promoter, Monsignor Rafael Larraín,[18] was also the director of rural Catholic Action. For several years he had been engaged in the formation and development of Catholic Action groups in the countryside. The new rural educational centers, although sponsored through an independent organization, became key bases for training rural leaders. Their vocational activities were closely tied up with Catholic Action ideas and principles. Thus Dominguez states, "Rural Catholic Action, in collaboration with the Institute of Rural Education, has undertaken to develop in the countryside an apostolic penetration according to the general perspectives of the Church"; [19] and "the Institute of Rural Education and Rural Catholic Action have gained experiences in the work of developing the community: through simple programs of development that permit the mobilization of all positive voluntary forces that dominate the rural milieu." [20] The three aspects of the educational program—technical, social, and intellectual—are synthesized in special courses for *delegados* or leaders.

Other important social development programs have been initiated in Brazil, Colombia, Panama, Guatemala, Venezuela, and the Altiplano region of Peru and Bolivia. The oft-cited program of Popular Promotion (*Promoción Popular*) in Chile [21] got its start through Church elites, but was later transferred to an agency of the Frei government. Similarly, the literacy program in the rural areas of Brazil—the Basic Education Movement—began as part of the Church's general programs of social development. During its most important phase, just prior to the coup of 1964, the Basic Education Movement was drawing major financial support from the government. In nearly every instance where the Church's initiatives have led to a program that required substantial financial support, public

[18] Rafael Larraín, not to be confused with the late Bishop Manuel Larraín of Talca, Chile.

[19] Dominguez, *El Campesino Chileno y la Acción Católica Rural,* p. 74, trans. Ivan Vallier.

[20] *Ibid.,* p. 75, trans. Ivan Vallier.

[21] Emanuel de Kadt, "Paternalism and Populism: Catholicism in Latin America," *Journal of Contemporary History,* II, No. 4, October, 1967, 96-97.

help has been achieved, or else the program has been secularized and made part of the total national effort.

The social development strategy attempts to fuse, or combine, solutions to felt needs among marginal peoples with Catholic Action principles. The clients are recruited through programs that hold a direct bearing on their social and material aspirations: opportunities for gaining leadership rewards, literacy training, and acquisition of technical emphases are cradled in a wider framework of religious ideas and doctrinal objectives. Militant laymen, rather than priests, carry out the field operations. But this does not alter the basic relation of these programs to the institutional Church. Through such devices as autonomous public corporations, and by the establishment of special linkages with governmental agencies, Church officials have been able to promote widely publicized programs of socioeconomic betterment that, in essence, are religious programs of influence, even though often defined as "pre-evangelism."

The earlier "missionary strategy" of the hard-core Catholic Action units is pushed to the background. Influence is not pursued in a direct, religious way, nor by an espousal of an official social encyclical line. Instead, the principles of augmenting influence are indirect, diffuse, and focused on the "whole man." Social, technical, and religious elements are fused into a series of functionally specialized programs that are deliberately organized to coopt the interests and loyalties of the marginal status groups.

The social development strategy has involved several important shifts in the Church's development. It has helped to combine an awareness of social needs with religious objectives, thus augmenting an image of a Church that is on the side of both change and the common people. Second, it has helped to reduce the outward, manifest confessional emphases of the Church, allowing it to establish new lines of contact and involvement with society. Finally, it has reduced the direct political involvements of the Church by channeling its activities into the economic, technical, and social spheres of society. All these processes have worked to extricate the Church from traditional strategies of influence. In the place of coalitions with conservative elites and opportunistic mobilizations of mass sentiment for the defense of Catholicism, there are emerging lines of interdependence with the culture of change, the felt needs of the common people, and the motivated layman. The model of religious action that is defined for the committed member is neither the fulfillment of formal sacramental involvements nor the aggressive, missionary activity of the Catholic Actionist, but an application of social and technical skills to the problems of population groups who hold an increasingly important place in the life of their respective societies.

The Cultural-Pastoral Strategy

Whereas the missionary and social developmental models are focused on augmenting the Church's influence among outside groups—workers, university students, *campesinos,* urban poor, etc.—the cultural-pastoral strategy is aimed toward a re-insertion of the Church's religious values into contemporary cultures and, at a second level, toward a revitalization of the religious commitments and sensibilities of the average member. In short, the cultural-pastoral strategy signifies a twofold development: on the one hand, an extension outward to cultural phenomena (symbols, general values, national goals, etc.) in terms of revised conceptions of society, change, and social integration; on the other hand, a revamping of the Church's internal life, especially with regard to the liturgy, preaching, member-to-member relations, pastoral principles, and sacramental practices.[22] Thus as the Church moves out and up in relation to society and culture, it moves in and down with regard to the problems of religious motivation and group relations. Both developments indicate an explicit effort to extricate the institutional Church from the political arena, yet by virtue of a corresponding emphasis on the values and aspirations of the people, and their legitimation at the cultural level, they do not constitute a withdrawal from society. It is especially significant that this strategy has emerged after the other two, with particular visibility since the early 1960s. Though certain initiatives were being taken before that time, the main thrusts have come since Vatican II.

This strategy moves the bishops into a central position of socioethical leadership. By virtue of his recognized place in both Church and society, the bishop becomes the basic link between the Church's new teachings and the collective problems of contemporary society. The few men who initiated this role, prior to Vatican II, were viewed as revolutionaries and destroyers of the Church. However, the general mood at the episcopal level has changed, with the result that a bishop is increasingly expected to assume responsibility for articulating the Church's social teachings and for bringing ethical pressures to bear on patterns of injustice, poverty, and social conflict. In these terms the bishop, or bishops as a collective body, disengage themselves from confessional interests and begin to assume a generalized role of cultural leadership, based on religious meanings and principles.

[22] The basic elements of the pastoral emphasis are described in Ivan Vallier, "Roman Catholicism and Social Change in Latin America: From Church to 'Sect,'" *CIF Reports,* III, May 3, 1964. See also Thomas G. Sanders, "The Priests of the People," Field Letter (TGS-11) to Richard C. Nolte, Institute of Current World Affairs, New York, N.Y., March 24, 1968.

The other, more internally focused, aspect of the cultural-pastoral strategy aims to restructure the parish church, create new forms of socio-religious solidarity, and increase the members' involvements in the Church's spiritual life. Opportunities are provided for new modes of religious expression, both within the framework of the liturgy and in smaller, homogeneous groups. Although particular programs hold varying degrees of importance for the transformation of local church life, I place within this development such activities as the liturgical reform, the new Bible study groups, some of the work of the *Cursillos de Cristianidad* (see Chapter Six), the house masses, team pastorates, and other specialized initiatives that attempt to foster a vigorous spiritual life among members in group settings. They all share, in one way or another, an emphasis on *religious* socialization. In the liturgy, for example, there is an attempt to overcome the traditional styles, such as formality, distance, and lay passivity. In turn, parishes are being restructured to provide, first, more opportunities for people of similar interests to worship together, and second, more opportunities for laymen to assume responsibilities for worship roles, administrative duties, and pastoral activities. Lay participation, collective and individual, is encouraged. Small-group principles are applied to study sessions and training retreats. In many of these efforts, one can discern the influence of the Protestants as a reference group. In fact, traditional Catholics are quick to point to the ways in which their Church is being "Protestantized."

The promotion of the cultural-pastoral strategy may be viewed as a product of several factors. On one level it reflects a recognition on the part of Church officials that any attempt to enter fully into the life of a modernizing, secular society requires a vigorous religious foundation among the rank and file. It is no longer possible to build insulating mechanisms between the Church and the outside world, nor to gain direct religious influence through specialized missionary corps, nor to assert religious dominance on the basis of traditional or political supports. Thus it is gradually being recognized that the only way to make a strong Church that is both in society and yet politically autonomous is to refashion the spiritual and religious life of its basic units, the person and the local church.

It appears that one of the main objectives, with regard to the individual Catholic, is to foster an internalization of religious control so that each person, in his daily encounters with secular society, will be able to withstand outside influences or, more ideally,[23] to actually exert a Christian influence on his nonbelieving associates. Through this emphasis on re-

[23] This theme is discussed at length in Chapter Six.

ligious motivation, the Church is shifting an important degree of religious control from the hierarchy, priest, and Catholic organizations to the individual actor. The assumption is made that if the rank-and-file member can be imbued with the basic religious values of progressive Catholicism and then integrate these with his other statuses, he can take a fully modern role in the non-Christian society without forfeiting his identity as a Catholic. Whether or not this process of resocialization can succeed without appreciable changes in the Church's views about lay charisma and the expression of religious feeling remains an open question.

The explicit efforts to re-align the Church's teachings and symbols with cultural phenomena at the higher levels of leadership are generated by the growth of non-Catholic and secular theories of society and frameworks of meaning. Marxism, nationalism, and synthetic Third World perspectives give primary attention to human values, ideologies of change, and principles of concrete action. These projections, especially when organized in terms of public slogans and definite visions of the future, carry an increasing influence among many social strata. Any attempt on the part of the Church to formulate a confessional, or Catholic, alternative to these persuasive appeals would only reinforce a traditional image. On the other hand, the adoption of a more universal posture, in which the needs and aspirations of all men are touched on, and especially those of the marginal strata, provides the Church leaders with a potential, if not actual, cultural basis for integrating religious values and social meanings.

MECHANISMS OF CHURCH INFLUENCE: EVOLUTIONARY PRINCIPLES

The three strategies that have been examined designate recent patterns of development. There are, however, two other adaptive strategies—the monopolistic and the political—that have played, and to some extent still play, significant roles in the activities of the Latin American Church. These latter two, along with the three treated above, are now analyzed together as the basis of a general evolutionary model of Church-society relationships (see Table 4.1). This model identifies five stages or Church systems, each distinguished by features that bear on the strategies and bases of control. I do not presume that this framework is complete. It is experimental and schematic, having the status of a series of ideal types.

For each stage or church type, as noted, the level of religious ambitions or church interest in religious control is "high." For present purposes, this is the only variable that remains stable. In more formal terms, "religious ambitions" is a constant. Rows 2, 3, and 4 underline the Church's

Table 4.1

Church Types and Influence Systems

Type	Stage I "Monopoly"	Stage II "Political"	Stage III "Mission-ary"	Stage IV "Social De-velopment"	Stage V "Cultural-Pastoral"
1. Level of Church ambitions	high	high	high	high	high
2. Church–society relation-ship	structural fusion	opposition and de-pendency	separation and controlled contact	public in-volvement	integrated autonomy
3. Major basis of influence	total insti-tutional complex	coalitions with tra-ditional elites	differenti-ated Catholic organiza-tions	social action programs among marginal strata	socio-ethical leadership
4. Secondary base of influence	ritual monopoly	clerical threats—withhold-ing of sacraments	ideological formation	mass media	local church
5. Target group	total population	aristocracy	workers and middle class	campesinos and urban poor	"other person"
6. Dominant ideology	territorial expansion and con-solidation	defeat political opposition	block or overcome seculariza-tion	provide religious basis for change	pluralist participa-tion
7. Religious action principle	diffuse control	defense of privilege	penetration of strategic secular spheres	solution of social problems	secular involve-ment
8. Priest's primary roles	ritual agent and civil servant	patron and/or politician	missionary and militant organizer	program developers and agents of change	pastor, and spiritual leader
9. Organiza-tional mode	segmental	coalitional	grass-roots missions	mobiliza-tion	national unity and coordi-nated microunits
10. Layman's role	ritual client	faithful follower	hier-archical auxiliary	partici-pating colleague	Christian-citizen

relation to society and the major basis of religious influence. The process of change in Church–society relations follows a path that begins with full fusion and becomes, at stage V, a posture I refer to as "integrated autonomy," i.e., the Church is fully differentiated from civil and secular supports and possesses corporate autonomy, but this differentiation implies neither separation from nor opposition toward society. Through collective forms of episcopal leadership, specially differentiated microunits, the full participation of the Christian-citizen in major roles, and a series of associational units, the Church gains an integral or organic relation to a changing society. These diverse activities and agencies of the Church in stage V are not, however, isolated and in competition with each other.

Row 9 specifies the major organizational mode for each stage: a segmental pattern for stage I, with subsequent shifts through the "coalitional," the "missionary," and the "mobilization" stages, up to stage V, wherein the Church combines national coordinative and developmental units with a variety of local and specialized microunits, some being task oriented, others being differentiated mainly for ritual and expressive purposes. These microunits reflect both the order of stratification in society as well as regional and local priorities.

Row 7 denotes the central principle of religious action or the basis of creating and focusing control strategies. "Diffuse control" efforts give way to a principle of action focused on the defense of traditional privileges. A very important break occurs between stages II and III, turning around the redefinition of society as a "missionary territory." By consequence, Church leaders turn from the task of trying to hold on to old guarantees to activities that are focused on reaching, contacting, and if possible coopting the loyalties or commitments of strategic status groups: urban workers, youth, the professionals, and rising political leaders. This stage began in Western Europe between 1870 and 1900, reaching its fullest expression in the decades of the 1920s, the Thirties, and the Forties.

General and specialized forms of Catholic Action occupy the key role so far as concrete structures are concerned. In Latin America, this shift got under way just prior to World War I, but with special sponsorship in the late Thirties through the mid-Fifties. By the time a Church reaches stage V, the key principle of religious action takes the form of full secular involvement on the part of the Christian-citizen, who integrates his religious role with that of political and social involvement in the differentiated structures of a complex society. It is the layman (row 10), not the priest or the bishop (row 8), who enters into the central arenas of society. The roles of the clergy are now focused more on fulfilling specialized spiritual roles, creating new forms of pastoral and communal life, and transposing traditional symbols into dimensions of social meaning. Note should be taken of the evolutionary shifts in the role of the layman, beginning with that of "ritual client" and reaching, in stage V, that of "Christian-citizen." He becomes the chief carrier unit of the religious system in its relations with society.

Changes in the Church's dominant ideology (row 6) pose more difficult tasks of identification and classification. Using ideology to cover the major ways in which Church elites define society, and how they are to relate to it, I make a distinction among ideologies that stress physical or territorial expansion, the defeat of political opponents, the containment of secularization, the provision of a religious framework for social change, and pluralist participation. The difference between the third and fourth stages is essentially a shift from a blocking strategy (i.e., to hold back forces of secular change) to that of a more innovative strategy that involves an acceptance of the inevitability of change, but tries to put a religious floor under it. At this point, the Church leaders turn from deliberate attempts to penetrate important and emerging functional spheres (the place of work, rising political movements, etc.) to the cultural sphere, and specifically to the national value system, in an effort to give the whole process of change at that level a religious coloring. It is at this point, as row 8 indicates, that the priest moves from his stage III role as a "militant organizer" to that of "agent of change." Once that position is developed and the process of change has taken on a direction that is religiously valued, the priest can move from the public sphere back into a central religious role, becoming a spiritual leader or pastor.

With these brief remarks as an introduction, each stage or church type may be summarily described:

Stage I. The monopoly stage is characteristic of those Churches which possess legal guarantees and political support as the "religion of the State," or the "established" religious system. In this stage the clergy are predominantly civil bureaucrats or employees of the state, and the hierarchy is legally subject to traditional forms of civil control and interference, such as the principle of patronage and the exercise of the *placet* or papal communications. The Church exercises influence through diffuse controls, privileged access to functional spheres, and indirectly, through the membership of its clergy in elite groups, and their connections with upper-status individuals.

Stage II. The "political" stage begins to emerge when the Church's formal guarantees and monopoly position are directly challenged and/or eliminated by opposing political forces. The key groups in the Church attempt to hold off these political changes and the ensuing ones by entering the political arena in alliance with conservative elites to support programs aimed at returning the society (and thus the Church) to its former condition. The Church makes short-term efforts to influence membership groups or elites who are moving toward the "left," but these efforts are primarily attempts to ensure the Church's continued control over territories and domination of social groups, the generation of moral influence and religious loyalties being distinctly secondary. In short, the Church assumes a posture of defense, seeing each infringement on its privileges as a wholesale attack on the religious system. Church elites concentrate their energies on political activity for strictly Catholic interests; but on the whole their efforts are not successful, and the status quo becomes progressively weaker, necessitating new forms of action.

Stage III. Given the demise of Catholic dominance and the failure of the political strategy to provide more than a temporary security, an alternative strategy is developed, i.e., a combination of developing parallel structures for purposes of insulating Catholics from secular forces and an outward but supervised missionary emphasis. Parallelism is a control strategy based on the development of diversified programs and activities that provide a set of Catholic structures in key functional arenas of society. The Church, as represented by the clergy and special missionaries, undertakes the sponsorship of Catholic trade unions, associations of mutual benefit, youth programs, professional societies, and schools for commercial and technical training. Since these Catholic structures function to keep loyal Catholics together in their various major statuses, the type of control afforded by parallelism is largely insulatory and protective rather than expansive. The Church-sponsored activities form a series of barriers, of varying degrees of permeability, between the non-Catholic secular world and the Catholic sectors of this same world; in addition, they give rise to a subculture that develops a variety of "Catholic" solutions to social, economic, and political problems.

However, protective-missionizing emphasis has not proved to be an effective long-range control strategy, for it tends to increase the "domineering" image of the Church by coopting laymen into an ever more visible authoritarian system. Moreover, it increasingly isolates the Church from the total society and thus reduces its potential capacity to speak for all men and on behalf of universal values. As it emerges, the prominence of the clergy as a link between the hierarchy and key spheres of secular activity diminishes, and the major *religious* responsibility for defending and extending Catholic values is placed on nuclear groups of laymen. These laymen, trained in special educational programs and ideological discussions, are intended to represent Catholic principles and values within the secular milieu. The missionary strategy involves a number of problems, including the desire for greater autonomy on the part of the laity involved, the danger of "contamination" by secular values, and weakened importance of sacramental life.

Stage IV. Given the difficulties involved for the Church in the insulative-parallel stage, another direction of development seems more attractive. The "social development" strategy concentrates on the initiation of social reform programs and the attempt to formulate a Catholic ideology of social change. Both these emphases tend to dissociate the Church from its earlier particularistic ties, giving it a generalized visibility and appeal to underprivileged groups. Catholic programs of social reform at the grass-roots level undertake to accelerate secular social change for the benefit of status groups that have heretofore been beyond the Church's influence or appeal. Moreover, by presenting a theology or ideology of change, the Church is able to free itself of its traditional association with conservative groups, and to identify itself with universal values acceptable to all modern groups. Churchmen become change agents, working to benefit society rather than specifically Catholic interests.

Stage V. In the cultural-pastoral stage, the Church develops a fourfold influence relationship with society. At the cultural level, it assumes the role of spokesman for a higher moral order, emphasizing the contemporary needs and relations of men. On the institutional level, it sponsors programs of public assistance and social development in areas or spheres not dealt with by the government. Both of these strategies are essentially continuations of approaches developed during stage IV. But in addition, the Church concentrates on activities at the local level in order to draw the individual into the Church as a fully committed and loyal layman. The goal of the control strategy is twofold: the formation of local Church units, which supply a focus for merging religious and social needs (and, incidentally, the locus for disseminating Church influence), and the socialization of a layman able to live in a pluralistic, secular society as a Christian and a citizen simultaneously—the key agent of Catholic influence. At this point, the role of the clergy is essentially that of a teacher-counselor, or a pastor who aids the members of his congregation without infringing upon their individual autonomy. Catholic influence at this stage is intended to be most pervasive, yet the most subtle, consisting largely in a set of values and normative principles to guide individual actions.

It must be recognized that these stages are, in essence, hypotheses about the course of development of religious influence. There is some partial evidence for their validity, but there is also evidence to demonstrate that a Church may be in transition between several stages at once, depending upon the region or level examined. The central theoretical importance of these hypotheses, however, is that they are directly related to the process of social change, and provide a means, even if only preliminary, for assessing the role of the religious factor in societal development in Latin America.

At least three conclusions can be drawn from my discussion of the evolutionary model of influence systems:

1. The Latin American Church is neither wholly traditional nor fully modern and revolutionary; instead, it embraces a highly complex range of competing, semiarticulated positions, strategies, and structures, all of which are directly related to the Church's interests in affecting behavior, consolidating loyalties, and placing a distinctive stamp on the course of institutional change.

2. The structures and strategies of influence that approach the "modern" pole are only realizable to the degree that a series of fundamental, qualitative changes take place in the Church's relations to cultural, social, and personal systems. These changes are the product both of developments in secular spheres and self-conscious efforts on the part of Church elites.

3. Any particular Church, whether marked out at the national or regional (intrasocietal) level, tends to be mainly positioned around one of the five types of influence systems, but with the possibility of secondary and tertiary tendencies representative of other types. These mixtures vary considerably and produce many tensions or imbalances, but these internal oppositions are only one source of instability. Each Church is also situated in at least three sets of pressures from the "outside": those stemming from the social revolution now under way in Latin America; those that are emerging from the efforts of other religious groups (especially the Protestants), both denominational bodies and Pentecostal sects; and those produced by the new directions of Church activity set by Vatican II.

Taking these three sets of extra-Church change stimuli as a baseline, certain patterns of emotional response and adaptation can be identified in relation to the five Church types. The broad, hypothetical distributions are presented in Table 4.2. These hypothesized patterns of religious response suggest that attempts to explain intra-Church tensions by reference to internal differences are not sufficient. These must be further related to outside forces: secular, Protestant, and Roman Catholic.

In this perspective, the "monopoly" Church takes on special importance, for it is expected to experience very deep sociopsychological strains that, in combination, push it very near to a "collective neurosis." The fear stemming from the political situation, plus the hostility bred by emerging value competition, overflows into the relations between the Latin American churchmen and the leaders of the post-Vatican movement of Church reform. Tensions from these relations also overlap with emotions

Table 4.2

Responses of Church Types to Outside Pressures

Types of outside pressure	Church Types				
	Monopoly	Political	Missionary	Social development	Cultural-pastoral
Socio-political revolution	Fear	Reactionism	Militancy	Public service	Normative leadership
Religious value competition	Primitive hostility	Suppression	Conflict	Competition	Cooperation
New directions in the International Church	Rebellion	Defensiveness	Criticism	Identification	Incorporation

bred by the other categories of threat. The over-all outcome can be nothing less than a highly anxious Church, incapable of sorting out priorities, immobilized except for reactionary bursts, and without the kind of internal cohesion and mutual confidence that can allow graceful defeats.

There can be no doubt that these emotional and sociopsychological undercurrents in the monopoly Church merge and are diffused rapidly into the major institutional spheres of the total society. Vicious circles become institutionalized as higher degrees of commitment become locked into coalitional and symbiotic patterns. Moreover, it is doubtful that a full-scale political revolution (even if possible under such conditions) would provide the basis for a new and flexible equilibrium. First of all, the new political movement would be likely to take strong sanctions against the Church as retributory compensation. This would only strengthen the inflexibility and reactionism of the defeated. Second, and no less important, a full revolutionary break could be expected to lead to a new type of religious authoritarianism which would by itself sustain and perhaps multiply the strength of negative emotional charges.

It is for these reasons (and others could be noted) that the burden of changing the monopoly Church and its closely related forms becomes a general problem of Latin American Church policy. These Churches cannot be simply eliminated or pushed to the margins of social life— too many psychological and structural involvements are embraced and focused by their ramified anchorages. Diplomacy, planned inducements, and the development of meaningful new roles will undoubtedly be needed.

THE CHRISTIAN REVOLUTIONARIES:
OLD OR NEW STRATEGY?

It will be obvious to some readers that I have studiously avoided mentioning a much-publicized, and perhaps growing, pattern of Catholic activity that is assuming a radical, revolutionary position in Latin America. Here, of course, I refer to the new groups and movements that are seeking to actively eliminate established structures of power and to create a totally new social order. Various terms are being used to identify these movements, e.g., "Christian revolutionaries," the "guerilla Church," "the new left," etc.[24] The participants and promoters of Christian-inspired revolutionary change, whether in society or in the power structures of the Church, take as positive referents certain themes in Vatican II documents (especially the concept of "servant Church," the responsibility of the Church for social justice and human life, and collegiality), as well as the more progressive statements emanating from recent episcopal councils, particular papal encyclicals (e.g., *Populorum Progressio,* 1967), and the speeches and writings of certain bishops and priests, including Dom Helder Camara (archbishop of Recife and Olinda in Northeast Brazil), Ivan Illich, and the late Camilio Torres. The negative referents with regard to the Church are conservative bishops, thoughtless and passive laymen, and the bureaucratically-inclined clerics. However, the evils within the Church serve only as a point of departure for taking up the evils of institutional life in the wider society. Famine, disease, illiteracy, corruption, and privilege are all part of a social order that has to be broken. This goal has given the Christian revolutionaries a concrete mission; one that can be legitimated in terms of basic Christian traditions.

[24] For further reference on the Catholic Left in Latin America, see Frederick C. Turner, *Catholicism and Political Development in Latin America,* Ms., 1968, especially Chapter IV: "Catholic Revolutionaries: Radicals or Avant-Garde?," pp. 161-218; Thomas G. Sanders, "Catholicism and Development: The Catholic Left in Brazil," in Kalman H. Silvert, ed., *Churches and States: The Religious Institution and Modernization,* New York, American Universities Field Staff, Inc., 1967, pp. 81-99; Thomas C. Bruneau, "How to Demoralize the Laity," *America,* June 22, 1968, pp. 789-91; "Les Problemes de L'Eglise au Bresil," Center of Intercultural Documentation, Cuernavaca, Mexico, *Document 68, 1969* [no author cited]; Manoel Cardozo, "The Brazilian Church and the New Left," *Journal of Inter-American Studies,* VI, 3, July, 1964, pp. 318-19; Germán Guzmán Campos, *Camilio: Presencia y Destino,* Bogotá, Colombia, Editores Publicidad, Servicios Especiales de Prensa, 1967; "Révolution, Violence, Communism: Dom Helder S'explique," *Informations Catholiques Internationales,* No. 315, July 1, 1968, pp. 4-7; and Thomas C. Bruneau, "Autonomy and Change in the Brazilian Church," Ms., 1969.

At the present time these revolutionary groups are involved in forming a general strategy, which may or may not be realized in actuality. Although a vague consensus exists about the need for revolutionary action against oppressive structures (domestic and foreign), a great deal of ambiguity, or at least disagreement, is evident in the definition of specific objectives, local tactics, and organizational bases. There is presently a strong internal conflict over the role of violence. Similar disputes appear to have emerged around the problem of Marxist collaboration and with regard to the choice of primary structural targets. Some of the discontinuities in focus and activity are probably bred by the diversity of backgrounds among the participants. It appears that the main membership of the groups is drawn from either specialized Catholic Action movements, especially student organizations, or from the stratum of intellectuals and professionals, particularly individuals who are involved in education, journalism, and developmental programs. These groups, in turn, are reinforced by a growing number of clergy and religious groups. At the apex stand a small, but highly visible, group of bishops who, quite obviously, do not see things with the same eyes. All these factors help to give the new movements diversity in outlooks and programmatic emphases.

The two main themes that keep coming to the surface as incipient bases of a general strategy are charismatic leadership and political action. The charismatic theme is displayed in the styles of leadership adopted by key figures, as well as in the kinds of emotional emphases followers exhibit toward these leaders. These charismatic elements are reinforced by a flat rejection of complex organizations and institutional forms. Ideal social relations are egalitarian, personalized, diffuse, and flexible. On the other hand, the political component is indicated in these movements' conception of action in society, namely direct, public action for the purpose of effecting radical changes in society, especially in the structures of economic, political, and military power. To act religiously, or in true keeping with Christian tradition and recent Church teachings, is to become a political man on behalf of the forgotten, the poor, and the oppressed. Thus the leaders of the underground legitimate their proposals for radical change by referring to the "prophetic tradition" in early Christianity. There is also a definite identification with the problems of all Third World peoples. Latin American societies are joined to those in Africa and Asia, since all are victims of an international power establishment, economic exploitation, and forms of neo-colonialism. These theological and ideological themes appear in most major speeches and current writings, and serve as the basic norms for local revolutionaries. In turn, various kinds of concrete situations are used to project these ideas and goals into the everyday life of the societies: e.g., a meeting of bishops becomes an opportunity to present a written manifesto for radical change; the dedication of a new cathedral or parish church prompts a public demonstration; a workers' strike stimulates letters of collegial support, some amounts of participative action, and the distribution of leaflets; a bishop's discipline of an innovator priest generates an immediate protest from laymen and a certain number of priests, sometimes leading to a long sequence of dramatic conflicts and divided sentiments. It is quite clear that these manifestations receive a press that is disproportionate to their actual importance. Even small incidents draw immediate publicity.

It may be that this growing wedge of Christian revolutionaries will gain a central position of power in the Church. Some observers judge that this is happening in Brazil, and perhaps in Argentina. In my judgment the key question is not whether they will become a central, and decisive, development within the Church but rather will their involvements in complex and highly-charged political issues revive traditional ecclesiastical ambitions which, in essence, imply that "Catholics have all the answers." If this occurs, religious cleavages and political cleavages will reinforce one another—a direction that can only exacerbate and prolong dissensions with societies that are already fragmented and hesitant. Consequently the Christian revolutionaries may be resurrecting an old strategy instead of developing a new one.

SUMMARY STATEMENT

Accretionary and abrupt changes in the fabric of Latin American societies have forced Church officials to recognize that traditional styles of leadership and religious control are not only self-defeating but also unsuitable for gaining a position of visibility and influence in contemporary life. A new type of organizational rationality is being applied in these circumstances, combining specialized leadership, selective lines of contact with marginal groups, the involvement of laymen in missionary endeavors, and new emphases on religious solidarity and associational strength. These initiatives have been examined both for their specific importance in freeing the Church from traditional adaptive styles and also for their interrelations as part of a more general evolutionary model of Church development. It is evident that some of the newer strategies are laying the foundations for a Catholicism that possesses structural autonomy, yet in addition produces positive outputs for the wider society.

The dimensions chosen to represent the evolutionary patterns underline a twofold conception of the relation of religion to society: first, that the Catholic Church (no less than other major world religions) does not lose, or graciously abandon, its interest in influencing, affecting, and guiding social action in society, but instead shifts its strategies for achieving those goals; second, that a religion, such as Catholicism, cannot be studied, appraised, and understood by limiting attention to the attitudes and behaviors of "the members" or those of the clergy, but must take account of multiple levels of thought, activity, and organization. Thereupon tensions arise, either between the Church and society or among sectors of the Church internally, because of the uneven ways in which particular levels of action undergo change. Interlevel or intersectorial leads and lags have the same theoretical importance in studies of religious systems as they do in investigations of economics and politics.

Church development is an integral part of social change and involves a number of special relationships with the wider situation. None of these is more important than the linkages that emerge between the Church and the political sphere. I have used the term integrated autonomy [1] to identify the basic relation of the emerging new Church to society. At the political level, this concept refers to the existence of a definite autonomy between the Church and political structures and, at the same time, support on the part of the Church for the over-all goals of national change and modernization. This ideal state of affairs is inherently problematic, first because the Church, even though it may have gained a new level of religious confidence and measures of internal solidarity, continually encounters threats and pressures that lead it to search for external help. In these uncertain situations, the support of friendly political groups becomes particularly attractive. Second, political movements and national parties are equally eager to extend their bases of legitimacy and influence, often looking to the hierarchy for sponsorship or endorsement. If the Church responds to these requests, it becomes implicated in partisan affairs, reducing the relationship of autonomy between the religious and political spheres. Several other problems arise in the Church's

CHAPTER FIVE

[1] See Table 4.1, p. 72.

The New Church and Political Processes

developmental process that interrupt the possibilities for the institutionalization of sustained autonomy. At the theological level, new emphasis is
being given to "worldly action" on the part of laymen. To fulfill their
vocation as good Catholics, they are admonished to value the temporal
sphere and to fuse religious and secular orientations. Yet the responsibility for realizing this subtly defined combination is left to the individual, with the frequent result that actions on behalf of the Church
and actions as citizens are mixed. Under certain circumstances this leads
to political engagements that competing groups define as Church sponsored. When this happens, the hierarchy becomes politically implicated
by default.

At another level, the priests continually find themselves in ambiguous
positions vis-à-vis the political sphere. In their attempts to facilitate social change through programs of community development, literacy work,
or experimental land reform projects, they initiate actions that have direct
and indirect political implications. Moreover, the diffuse meaning of the
priest's status in Latin American societies gives any activity with which
the clergy is connected a definite ecclesiastical meaning. What begins as
a project for "the benefit of the people," and for which they are made
responsible, quickly turns into a general symbol of Church involvement in
political issues. The Church is accused of stirring up agitation among the
masses or trying to dominate programs of social and economic betterment. If these political meanings define the situation, the Church finds
itself back into politics and the whole principle of religious autonomy is
weakened.

These examples suggest that the Church stimulates many kinds of
political meanings and is easily aligned with one side or another as it
attempts to shift its bases of influence away from traditional patterns
to more modern ones. But there are also a number of trends and changes
that are helping to depoliticize the Church, i.e., helping to provide it
with a relationship to society that approaches a pattern of integrated autonomy: (1) the post-Vatican Church's emphasis on socioethical leadership, internationally and nationally, (2) the growth of national and
regional episcopal conferences that enhance the Church's collective impact of socioethical pronouncements, (3) the growth of bureaucracy in
the Church, (4) the growth of Christian Democratic parties, and (5) the
growth of outside, extranational, sources of financial and clerical support.

I consider these important enough to deserve extended discussion. My
assumption is that the basic significance of the emerging new Church
for political development is not to be assessed in terms of whether it
gives direct endorsement to "democratic values," or stimulates "political
participation" of marginal groups, or legitimizes national political offices.

Significant here is the degree to which it gains autonomy from central political arenas while at the same time providing religious support for the general values of development, change, and collective achievement.

An increase in emphasis on socioethical leadership. The Roman Catholic Church's international character provides it with a special potential for articulating and symbolizing universal values. This potential has not always been exploited; instead the Church has tended to use its international capacities in the service of confessional goals. This is beginning to change, receiving particular impetus from the time of John XXIII.[2] Although his *Mater et Magistra*[3] and *Pacem in Terris*[4] carried on the themes of earlier social encyclicals, they also included emphases on the Church's role as servant to all men, especially the support of values and goals that inhere in the human situation. Paul VI extended these emphases in *Populorum Progressio*.[5]

But this recent shift to socioethical leadership has occurred at other levels than that of the papacy. Many bishops and priests were already assuming this role in local situations. Instead of using their office and prestige as bases for promoting confessional goals and mobilizing commitments to sacramental participation, the stress has been on the problems of the poor, the importance of human freedom and dignity, and the sacredness of the value of social justice. In these allocutions the "Catholic" elements of religious meaning are subordinated to values and goals that are universally sacred. Political issues are implied in these endorsements, of course. But they do not necessarily politicize the Church, first, because the Church lays the responsibility for the implementation of changes on members as citizens; second, because these values hold a charisma and legitimation on many bases other than Christian beliefs or Catholic theology. The important point is that the Church, as a religious system, articulates them in conjunction with other sponsors. Paul VI's visit to the United Nations in 1965 was not only a special kind of diplomatic event, but symbolized a new kind of mutual complementarity between an international political body's emphasis on human welfare and an international religious body's concern with human welfare.

The solidification of symbolic linkages between religious leadership and human welfare enhances the charisma of both, helping to bring sacred meaning to the latter and secular legitimacy to the former. This is not simply arid double-talk, but points to a crucial aspect of the total developmental process. However, the degree to which this linkage is in-

[2] 1958-1963.
[3] May 15, 1961.
[4] April 11, 1963.
[5] March 26, 1967.

stitutionalized or sustained depends, in no small degree, on the ways in which local bishops develop their leadership roles, both in their dioceses and as a collegial body.

The bishop in the Roman Catholic Church holds an interesting socio-logical position.[6] He is an ecclesiastical monarch, invested with powers of a sacramental, juridical, administrative, and pastoral nature. In the regular activities of the diocese, he is final decision maker, judge, and executive. He can transfer clergy at will, commission new churches to be built, give sponsorship to lay initiatives, dispense funds (if available) to charity and good causes, and issue pastoral letters that encourage or chastise the laity. The bishop also confirms the youth of the Church, ordains the seminarians to the priesthood, and issues special dispensa-tions in certain matters related to moral doctrine. He is, in the broadest sense of the term, a local religious king.[7]

In Latin America, bishops are often severely criticized for particular actions and considered insignificant in relation to other elites, but the episcopal office continues to possess an important structural position. Al-though particular bishops may be attacked, the office is not. In all the recent protests that radical Catholics have made against "the Church," none, so far as I know, has pressed for the elimination of the episcopal office; instead, it is the incumbents who are regarded as incompetent and naïve.[8] Given this distinction between the man and the position, it is quite clear that the episcopate takes on considerable importance in ap-proaching the relations between Catholicism and social change in Latin America.

In his relations with the outside world, several roles are open to a bishop. He may, for instance, assume the role of ceremonial leader in public celebrations and political assemblies. This is a ritual role, geared

[6] The nature of the episcopal office and the norms that are to govern episcopal leadership are systematically developed in the "Decree on the Bishops' Pastoral Office in the Church," promulgated October 28, 1965. For a complete text of the decree, see Walter M. Abbott, *The Documents of Vatican II*, trans. ed. Joseph Gallagher (New York: Guild Press, 1966), pp. 396-429.

[7] On the formal definitions of the rights and duties of the episcopal office, see "Bishops and the Government of Dioceses," in *Canon Law. A Text and Commentary*, 4th rev. ed., eds. T. Lincoln Bouscaren, *et al.* (Milwaukee: The Bruce Publishing Co., 1966), pp. 176-90.

[8] This pattern is apparently general throughout the Church. A comparative study which I am now completing on lay developments in dioceses of France, Chile, and the United States indicates that laymen, in their evaluations of leadership problems and elite competencies, make a clear separation between the office and incumbents. For a first report on this study, consult Ivan Vallier and Rocco Caporale, "The Roman Catholic Laity in France, Chile, and the United States: Cleavages and De-velopments," *Information Documentation on the Conciliar Church*, Nos. 68-7 and 68-8, February 18 and February 25, 1968.

to the enhancement of communal identification. He may, on the other hand, play the role of the moral guarantor, making it his business to see that nothing contrary to the teachings of the Church is allowed to gain legitimacy in the surrounding society, e.g., legislation permitting divorce. This inevitably leads to political involvements or to the political role, since many proscriptions authored by the Church carry implications for civil life, personal freedom, and social welfare. Consequently these issues fall increasingly within the domain of the nation state, rather than having the status of religious rules. A third role that a bishop may take vis-à-vis the wider society is that of socioethical spokesman, or the creator and propagator of values and ethical principles that bear a positive relevance to all men as human beings. Instead of promoting confessional interests or performing rituals during community events, he articulates norms and ideas that stimulate all men to value freedom, preserve liberty, promote the community's well being, and augment the principles of social justice. This latter role, if judiciously performed, may assist the formation of an underlying value consensus.

This socioethical emphasis differs considerably from either the ritual leadership role or the protopolitical role of the moral guarantor. By speaking for and within a universal value framework—"all men," "all times"—the basis of meaning is shifted from both confessional interests of the Church (Catholic values) and local ideological issues (right versus left, etc.). This does not imply, however, that the socioethical role carries no political implications. Certainly it does, in that it identifies a set of oughts that, in order to be realized, require basic structural changes in society. But this political dimension does not identify a particular party or ideological group as the single mechanism of change or as the major conservator of tradition. If, as in certain recent instances, bishops identify a particular group, such as the landowners, the rich, or the military, as the political culprit, then the socioethical position slips from the level of collective meaning to that of a specific change ideology.[9] If this occurs, the Church is likely to become implicated in short-term political involvements, as it did earlier in the support of the conservatives.

There appears to be a thin line, perhaps too thin, between what I refer to as the socioethical role and the politicization of the Church toward the side of fundamental structure change, or even revolution. Is there a difference between bishops who articulate values of social justice, freedom from oppression, and "love for neighbor," and those who emphasize a redistribution of wealth, revolutionary modes of change, and an end to

[9] A clear example of this type of emphasis is found in Brazilian Bishop Antonio Batista Fragoso's statement, "Evangelio y Justicia Social," *Cuadernos de Marcha* (Montevideo), XVII, No. 9 (1968), pp. 12-20.

political repression? Both call attention to an unsatisfactory state of affairs; both indicate a need for change; both stress ideal, if not utopian, models of the good society. Yet in the first instance, the foundations of the Christian belief system can be drawn on to give meaning and universal status to the prescriptions; in the second case, however, there is advocacy of particular means and an indirect, if not direct, assignment of political guilt. Whereas the first level of articulation identifies the elements of a value system that has a religious base, the second endorses a set of political strategies.

The role of the episcopal conferences, national and regional. The chances that the bishop's role of socioethical leader will gain predominance over other action styles are increased by the emergence of extra-diocesan episcopal conferences through which bishops may speak collectively. So long as the responsibility for articulating socioethical values is left to the individual bishop, and, at a higher level, to the infrequent statements of the pope, the possibilities for giving these values national meaning are reduced. The national and regional episcopal conferences can function as important intermediate units between the papacy and the local diocese. In short, the episcopal conferences stand to play a key role in helping to institutionalize the Church's emerging emphasis on "above-politics" influence.

In Latin America, both a regional (or continental) episcopal council (*Consejo Episcopal Latinoamericano*) [10] and national episcopal conferences exist (such as the National Conference of Brazilian Bishops and the National Conference of Chilean Bishops). These overarching structures do not possess authority to make binding decisions over local bishops, but they do function as coordinative and communicative centers, as bases of planning and institutional development and, more important, as platforms from which broad statements of religious values and ethical principles can be made.

All these units gained new degrees of legitimation and authority from the Vatican II Council. In the Decree on the Bishops, special attention is given to the nature and functions of episcopal conferences. Bishops are admonished to establish collegial structures at the national level, to meet frequently in terms of common problems, and to develop harmonious and collective bases of leadership.[11] In a chapter of the Decree, entitled "Concerning the Cooperation of Bishops for the Common Good

[10] The Latin American Episcopal Council (CELAM) was established in 1955. Its general secretariat is located in Bogota, Colombia. For details on its organization, special departments, and activities see *Latinamerican Episcopal Council*, Bogota, General Secretariat of CELAM, Apartado Aereo 5278, C. 1967.

[11] Abbott, ed., *The Documents of Vatican II*, Art. 37, p. 425.

of Many Churches," the features and purposes of the national episcopal conferences are specified. An episcopal conference is defined as a "kind of council" through which the bishops of a region or country develop and exercise a collective pastoral office as a means of promoting "that greater good which the Church offers mankind." [12]

Although many special problems afflict these emerging episcopal conferences, including the problem of gaining the support of local bishops and the difficulties of translating plans into programs, their main function with respect to the relation of the Church to society, and more specifically the political realm, is the creation of opportunities for the bishops to formulate and articulate "wider norms and symbols" from an extrapolitical and extralocal base. It is through these episcopal conferences, and the special agencies that have been created within them, that the Church can begin to assert a religious leadership that is, on the one hand, directly relevant to the secular sphere and the processes of change but, on the other hand, is outspoken in disengagement from particular situations and partisan interests.

The important fact is that these pronouncements favoring basic social change emanate from the bishops as a collective body at the national and continental levels. It is this collective aspect that helps to link religious ideas to the problems of economic and political development. Although some bishops do not endorse these messages, this does not detract from their over-all meaning and influence. The 1962 pastoral statement of the Chilean bishops is not an indicator of episcopal unity so much as it is an indicator of a new relationship between the Church and social change. It is equally important to note that the document or pastoral letter places the responsibility for action on the individual Christian:

The Christian, to be truly so, must take a stand regarding these reforms, to be sure that social structures be such that they allow the lower income layers of the population a greater share in the fruits of the productive process. To this end, Christian man must favor the institutions for social vindication and, if necessary, participate in the operation of these institutions.[13]

The "bureaucratic" trend in Church organization. The growth of bureaucracy and specialized staff roles in formal organizations is often viewed in a negative light. Bureaucracy conjures up images of graded statuses, formal rules, administrative red tape, and impersonal relations

---

[12] *Ibid.*, Art. 38, p. 425.
[13] Quoted from "Latin America's Plea for Vast Social Change," in *The Church in the New Latin America*, ed. John J. Considine (Notre Dame, Ind.: Fides Publishers, Inc., 1964), pp. 47-48.

with clients. These are, perhaps, inevitable components of bureaucratic growth, but they do not tell the whole story, particularly in the case of the emerging new Church in Latin America. The hypothesis I shall develop in this section is that the growth of flexible and specialized organizational patterns in the administrative and professional centers of national Church life increases the Churches' capacities to remain an autonomous and religiously focused system. The consolidation and integration of administrative, coordinative, and staff functions provide Church officials with an organizational capacity to initiate and sustain autonomous programs of activity and influence. By gaining this capacity, the probabilities of a turn to political support or the forming of short-term crisis coalitions are lessened.

The trend toward bureaucratization is being augmented by a number of special developments: (1) the increased salience of the total nation, rather than regions or localities, as the unit of reference in the definition of collective tasks; (2) the rising functional importance of the national episcopal conferences as deliberative and decision-making units; (3) the increased need for research, planning, and administrative specialists as the churches move away from a reactive style of problem solving to that of selective programming; (4) the growing importance of the mass media in Church operations, spurring an emphasis on technical specialists, budgetary efficiency, and centralized decision making; (5) the post-Vatican pressures, felt in national Churches, to translate pronouncements and decrees into recommendations that form the basis for policy decisions in the local Churches; and (6) the proliferation of diverse initiatives of a missionary or social-development nature that need to be coordinated, supervised, and related to one another. These developments are stimulating Church officials to promote organizational emphases and administrative centers that are not tied directly to the diocesan and parochial levels. Instead, a whole new range of communication networks, specialized agencies, and professional elites (clerical and lay) is emerging that is oriented to the rhythms, trends, and problems of the total society. Local programs are initiated as part of a wider scheme of plans and priorities.[14]

---

[14] The growth of bureaucracy carries at least two consequences, other than strengthening the Church's autonomy in society: (1) It provides a structural basis for developing collective strength at the episcopal level, thus increasing the bishops' capacity to function as socioethical leaders; (2) it provides an organizational framework within which local movements and experimental programs can be given flexibility and freedom. This latter point bears special emphasis, since I hold that the development of local community patterns, e.g., around the parish, depends on the existence of a wider system of coordination and leadership. Otherwise dispersion, rather than development, occurs. This is important in light of the fact that one of the basic problems in the traditional Church stemmed from its centrifugal tendencies.

The bureaucratic, nationalizing forces in the Church's organized activities are a decisive reversal of the local, segmental tendencies of the traditional Church. Although bishops remain the juridical, pastoral, and administrative heads of their own dioceses, most of the basic problems that the Church faces vis-à-vis society cut across and over the top of these local units. Dioceses are not passed by, but rather linked to one another or tied, in specialized ways, to wider initiatives.

These changes expectedly stimulate negative responses among traditionally oriented bishops. They view the diocese as "the Church" in a given territory, with the papacy as the only outside referent. The "new men" who promote empirical research, national pastoral plans, social programs, and coordinative ties are defined as usurpers, interlopers, and bureaucrats. Yet it is precisely the absence of either interdiocesan linkages or a national perspective that reduces the traditional diocese's capacities to extricate itself from both local political pressures and short-term adaptive measures. Each bishop proceeds to shape policies in response to local conditions rather than as part of a wider national enterprise. Bishops are only beginning to realize that extradiocesan structures do not rob them of episcopal authority but rather relieve them of many of the day-to-day pressures that have tended to interfere with pastoral interests. The growth of specialized, nonepiscopal structures at the national level actually increases the possibilities for the emergence of the bishop's role as a spiritual and pastoral leader.

The output to the wider society is at least twofold, depending on the perspective one adopts. On one level, the growth of bureaucratic and organizational solidity helps to keep the Church differentiated from the political arena. The output is indirectly positive, at least in my judgment, since it places the Church out of the reach of politicians who may need it to help legitimate their position and, in turn, it places administrative specialists and professionals or technicians in decision-making roles, thus institutionalizing criteria of problem solving that tend, on the whole, to be apolitical. Moreover, the growth of professional specialists and the institutionalization of planning procedures brings a long-range time span into the operations of the Church, once again lessening the chances that short-term political maneuverings will be chosen as the principal adaptive mode.

The bureaucratic trend in the Church does not represent an exclusive, determinant process that automatically interferes with expressive, communal, and prophetic forms of Catholic life.[15] Instead it needs to be

[15] I do not see the "bureaucratic" and "communal" elements as contradictory or as opposing tendencies but as specialized developments occurring at different levels within the total Church.

viewed as a specialized structural development that answers to only one set of problems in a modernizing Church. It is not the whole thing, nor a sign of retrogression, but actually one of many conditions for religious development.

The role of Catholic-based reform parties (e.g., Christian Democratic parties). Considerable amounts of attention are presently being given to the political and economic significance of Christian Democratic parties in Latin America.[16] The Catholic-related but nonconfessional parties have begun to achieve national prominence as forces for national development, especially the *Partido Democrática Cristiano* in Chile and the Social Christian-COPEI (*Comité de Organización Política Electoral Independiente*) in Venezuela. Because of their potentialities for combining Catholic thought with programs of social reform, as well as their ideologies of a "third way" (neither capitalist or communist), these parties, under conditions of party unity and strong leadership, have been able to make very important inroads in the middle classes and among sectors of the workers. Williams suggests that the relative weakness of some Christian Democratic parties, such as the one in Brazil, is not due only to the general conditions of the political situation, e.g., party fragmentation and regionalism, but also to the absence of "right-wing" Catholic parties that could provide Catholic conservatives with a focused base of identity and action.[17] In the absence of such parties, conservatives and progressives compete within the Christian Democratic organization, resulting in a loss of direction and power in the wider situation.

One issue that has not been received sufficient attention in discussions about Catholic reform parties is the latent role they can play in helping to institutionalize a progressively oriented but nonpolitical Church, as well as providing political arenas for Catholic laymen who opt for a progressive political type of worldly action but still want to remain involved in the Church. Strong and progressive Christian Democratic parties serve a twofold function under these circumstances: (1) they act as a buffer between the Church and the political arena; (2) they serve as a safety valve by providing a meaningful political arena for laymen who maintain Catholic orientations but pursue a politics of reform and change.

The significance of the Christian Democratic parties for both religious and political developments is found in the fact that both the "new Church" and the Christian Democratic parties represent aspects of a

[16] For a comprehensive description of the ideologies, goals, and programs of Christian Democratic parties in Latin America, see Edward J. Williams, *Latin American Christian Democratic Parties* (Knoxville, Tenn.: The University of Tennessee Press, 1967).

[17] *Ibid.*, pp. 246-47.

more general process of institutional change. Whereas the emerging new Church involves a direction of differentiation between religion and politics, the Christian Democratic parties embody a direct fusion of Catholic ideas and politics. Moreover, the Church's capacity to extricate itself from politics depends in large measure on the degree to which the Christian Democratic movement succeeds in achieving political identity and competitive political strength.

How does this twofold process begin, and what are some of the conditions of its progress? Two statuses are involved: those of the clergy and of the laity. With respect to the clergy, the most important factor is a turn away from public and political roles to those that emphasize socio-pastoral leadership. Religious ideas and priestly status are applied to the development of the social and ethical content of Christian beliefs. This does not mean that the priest withdraws interest from society, retreating into some type of otherworldly meditation, but rather transmits to laymen, in religious settings, the social implications of religious teachings.

The laity, on the other level, are stimulated to initiate political action in the world in line with the social encyclicals and other recent teachings of the Church. Instead of remaining tied to conservative political views, on the one hand, and the authority of the priest, on the other, laymen begin to recognize that they, rather than the official Church, constitute the basic agents of political influence. This independent political role for the layman, on behalf of social change, is in part a byproduct of the Catholic Action movement which, in religious terms and under the sponsorship of bishops, orients laymen to the world. However, this engagement with the world inevitably stimulates a latent political tendency. Since this cannot be expressed within the episcopally controlled Catholic Action movements, the importance of political units that are Catholic related but fully linked to the wider political system becomes evident.

Is the rise of a reform-type Catholic party a condition for the long-term development of the new Church in Latin America? I suggest that it is, otherwise the latent political impulses that the theologies of the progressive Church stimulate become fused with Church-sponsored movements and organizations. If this happens, the Church re-enters politics via a two-stage sequence. First, the enthusiastic, progressive, and politically oriented lay movements begin to take sides in the central arenas of the total political system. By these actions, the Church becomes directly implicated in a political position on the left. Since this inevitably creates intense conflict and anxiety within the Church, the hierarchy is certain to reject the politicized groups or silence them. When this happens the Church swings back to a "neutral position" (or noninvolvement) which is equivalent to a legitimation of the status quo. In short, a cycle of political involvement on the left breeds a new cycle of political involvement on the right. This is essentially the sequence that took place in Brazil between 1962 and 1964: movements of a political nature which were identified with Church programs became directly, and increasingly, involved in the politics of the left. This, in turn, implicated the hierarchy in leftist politics, stimulating in turn a variety of pressures from conservative groups within the Church and in the wider society. In order to dissociate itself from a particular political position, the hierarchy took steps (or allowed others to initiate action) to bring the leftist political tendencies to a halt. This occurred at the same time of the military coup and by consequence pushed the main center of gravity in the Church "to the right."

Had a viable, developing Christian Democratic party with reform policies existed in Brazil during the early Sixties, many of the political tendencies in the Catholic movements may have been channeled into party activities. As it was, the politicized Catholics, operating in structures associated with the Church, went directly into politics and were perceived as dragging the "whole Church" with them. The response of the hierarchy inadvertently turned the Church back to the conservative side.

Isolation of the conservatives—the role of outside resources. The Latin American Church is receiving substantial amounts of resource assistance from outside agencies, e.g., the German Bishops' Fund, North American episcopates, and such governments as the United States. Some Latin Americans view this outside help as negative, arguing (1) that financial aid spurs bureaucracy and institutional structures, rather than living Christian communities, (2) that financial and personnel assistance are sources of nonproductive, foreign ideas having no meaning and relevance to local needs, and (3) that these outside interests are essentially new forms of "religious colonialism" and political imperialism, and as such they damage the capacities for the development of an authentic Christianity in Latin America.[18]

These charges undoubtedly have some validity; it is rare indeed that assistance comes without strings attached or that outside ideas have no disturbing implications. But the negative consequences can be easily overemphasized. In fact, it appears that outside assistance carries several significant implications for the process of Church development. Of these, none is more important than the "freedom" these outside resources provide the "new Church" vis-à-vis the traditional Catholic elites. When they gain assistance from the outside, the progressives do not have to be concerned so much about the reactions of the right, e.g., influential lay-

[18] For a pointed statement of this view, see Ivan Illich, "The Seamy Side of Charity," *America,* January 21, 1967, pp. 88-91.

men. If, on the other hand, the Church had to rely on its own constituency for funds or beg from the government, it would not only be subjected to a number of traditionalizing constraints and obligations but also would become open to new forms of politicization.

Wherever the purse of the Church is dependent on either the wealthy or the government, it loses its capacity for social-cultural autonomy and for innovation. The Latin American case is very special. On the one hand, it draws very little financial support from the voluntary contributions of the members. On the other hand, new programs and increased numbers of personnel require financial resources.

INSTITUTIONAL DOMINATION VERSUS RELIGIOUS
SUPPORT OF SECULAR ENDEAVORS

The types of trends that facilitate the growth of autonomy between the Church and the political sphere have been described; now it is possible to take up the nature of the Church's changing relationship to the cultural and institutional levels of social life. I shall examine two issues: (1) the traditional emphasis of the Church on total normative responsibility, or its broad ambitions for ordering social behavior and institutions; and (2) the nature of the changes that occur as a Church shifts from a broad institutional interest to that of fostering values and meanings within which diverse types of social action may be related.

The Ambition to Determine Order in all Spheres of Society

Roman Catholicism is a religion that aspires to be a total institution, being willing to supply and perpetuate religious norms in all institutional areas: economic institutions, political institutions, social and educational institutions, family life, etc. Detailed concepts and regulatory principles are proffered for the entire range of institutional activity. Prescriptions, proscriptions, admonitions, rubrics, rules, and categories have flowed from the Church to help it dominate, influence, and otherwise order the human world. There is a Catholic position on nearly everything: property, labor unions, war, citizenship, intercourse, parenthood, education, welfare, crime, prices, interest, marriage, divorce, etc.

The Church has inherited these broad interests from earlier ages when, in fact, it functioned as the major (and often only) potential agency of normative creation and cultural control. But the perpetuation of this orientation in contemporary society has two negative consequences, one for its own charisma or prestige and one for the processes of change in society:

1. Blanket ambitions undercut the Church's general legitimacy and influence because its normative prescriptions (or proscriptions) are continually subjected to the test of empirical evidence and collective experience and come into conflict with deeply institutionalized values of personal freedom, individual choice, and privacy. So long as it persists in trying to order life by Catholic standards in spheres that are not defined as strictly religious, it will continue to experience this loss of legitimacy and authenticity.

2. Of even greater importance for the process of change and development in society is the traditional Church's total approach to institutional life, which frequently imbues potentially modernizing ventures and roles with a traditional basis. Its emphases distort and confuse norms that are specialized in relation to key functions, e.g., technology, professional education, administration, legal developments, etc. Religious considerations enter into decisions that are best made according to nontheological criteria. Thus, the "Catholic technician" should not have to look at his materials and evaluate the procedures for their shaping and manipulation in terms of Catholic categories, but strictly in terms of technical criteria and technical considerations. Similarly the Catholic social scientist should not be under burden to fuse his observations on society and to evaluate his findings in terms of Catholic canons of inference or Catholic notions of the role of knowledge in the formation of social policy.

One of the most critical shifts in this whole process of autonomization occurs when churchmen begin to recognize that their religious expertise does not provide them with competence to dictate behaviors in nonreligious spheres. But this leads only to anxiety and defensiveness if they do not, at the same time, begin to feel that new degrees of charisma or status can be achieved through religious ideas on other bases. The role of socioethical leader, or a position above politics, is one of the bases on which this transition is made. Churchmen, both bishops and priests, have tended to be secular men, in that they judged themselves competent to provide authoritative norms and direct advice on events in all spheres of society: economics, politics, education, and law. But as these arenas of activity become more specialized and professionalized, churchmen's views are shown deficient, and they have had to live with the embarrassments that their incompetencies produce. Although the Church may hold a set of broad theories about the nature of economic growth or property rights, these are not equivalent to a detailed model involving fiscal reform, investment priorities, and international trade. This is not to say that priests tried to be professional economists, but they have tended to behave as though this was their business.

This goal of institutional comprehensiveness is gradually giving way to a theory of religious specialization, wherein the Church, rather than trying to project its values into all spheres, cultivates particular competencies.[19] Once this specialized role of the Church is recognized, churchmen begin to re-examine the basic principles of faith and the nature of the general symbols that can give meaning and direction to all aspects of social life. This helps them to abandon the institutional realms of secular society, at least in a direct way, in favor of a more cultural and symbolic role. The sociological process is twofold: (1) an extraction process, or a moving away from concerns with particular role systems and regulative norms in nonreligious spheres; and (2) a re-fusing or reintegrative process that begins to connect the religious realm with the broader levels of cultural meaning and beliefs.

These changes undoubtedly depend on a general development in cultural phenomena and a higher degree of specialization among the elites that create and foster cultural patterns. The dominant pattern in Latin America is the projection of Catholic religious conceptions and values into nonreligious cultural domains. Vekemans, in an exceptionally important essay,[20] describes this religious dominance, arguing that a general cultural mutation must take place if modernization is to occur. He proposes what is an essentially political solution to this problem.

In order for a cultural mutation to take place, Latin American societies need to be integrated economically, culturally, and socially. If the continent achieves these integrative ties, including a consensus on long-range priorities and developmental strategies, the chances for productive exchanges with wider systems are greatly increased.[21] In other words, a cultural mutation requires the formation of a frontier space that functions as both an arena for the mixing of the old and the new and as a specialized source of new norms which, subsequently, pass over into the bounded unit—Latin America. Through integration, or the mutual alignment of interests and collective goals, Latin America would take on the characteristics of a system that could be regulated and influenced by new values. The lack of integration, on the other hand, leaves too many apertures, and preserves too many local and insulated centers of autonomy. These patterns inhibit an over-all orientation to common goals and interests, and correspondingly, reduce the possibility for cultural learning to take place.

This is a persuasive, but I think rather utopian, argument. Furthermore

[19] This emerging position is expressed in the "Pastoral Constitution on the Church in the Modern World," Chapter IV, "The Role of the Church in the Modern World," pp. 238-48 in Abbott, ed., *The Documents of Vatican II.*

[20] Roger E. Vekemans, "Economic Development, Social Change, and Cultural Mutation in Latin America," in *Religion, Revolution and Reform,* eds. William V. D'Antonio and Frederick B. Pike (New York: Frederick A. Praeger, Inc., 1964), pp. 127-42.

[21] *Ibid.,* p. 142.

it tends to release the Church from a principal responsibility to help actuate a cultural mutation. Although it is to be noted that Vekemans, through recent efforts, has ably promoted the Church as an agency of Latin American integration, this has created a whole series of new problems within the hierarchy. Against Vekemans's model or suggestion, I would give more emphasis to the role that a religious organization, such as the Church, could play in the process of cultural mutation.

The Potential Capabilities of the Church in Fostering a Cultural Mutation

The Church possesses the formal structure or institutional bases for facilitating resocialization and cultural mutation. Four particular avenues are open:

1. By reason of its relation to and involvement in the supernatural or nonempirical realm, the Church's idea men—theologians, intellectuals, theoretically inclined bishops—are provided with nearly unlimited possibilities for creating and transmitting new categories of meaning, thought, and judgment. To be effective, these attempts must hold some integral ties with prevailing cultural orientations and expectations; effectiveness is greatly dependent on the degree to which cultural innovations are indigenous. But it is at this level of the symbolic and the conceptual that major breakthroughs are needed. Some of these have occurred around such themes as "the Christian revolution," the notion of "worldly action" and the sacredness of the secular. But the general stream has remained quite thin and fragmented. Moreover most of the sources of these new images and concepts are non-Latin American, thus subject to considerable degrees of depreciation in meaning and relevance for the average member or priest.

2. The Church's status hierarchy and its system of authority, and thus the control of the local priest, do not depend on the will of the people. This means that the priest, providing that he is assured of support from his bishop, can take definite stands or promote new perspectives and norms without having to worry (at least to the degree of his free Protestant counterpart) about losing his job or having his legitimation withdrawn. The Church is so structured that the local authority figure can take independent stands. Whether he does or not varies with the situation. Most important is that the potential is there as the institutions of authority and leadership stand.

3. The Church possesses diverse and specialized mechanisms for reaching into the motivational levels of personality functioning, e.g., the confession, the mass, parochial schools, retreats, lay associations (Third Orders, as an instance), and the like. All these mechanisms are potentially instruments of thought control and religious influence, but may, in the majority of instances, simply help to perpetuate a set of general and traditional habits of thought and action. Again, the crucial issue is whether or not these mechanisms are used for re-

shaping motivation or serve only as means of increasing conformity and in-volvement in traditional Catholicism.

4. The Church, as organization or bureaucracy, holds a capacity for various kinds of coordinative and integrative roles. Whether attention is given to the national level, to that of the region (province or territory), or to the diocese, various types of integrative tasks can be performed. These capacities are es-pecially critical in periods when attempts are being made to revamp or alter basic religious outlooks and cultural values. If certain types of activities are deemed essential for carrying through a phase of resocialization, then it is quite beneficial if these can be planned and coordinated in terms of schedules that meet the requirements of particular local conditions, yet give the whole enterprise a unity and direction. Sometimes this is attempted, as with the recent liturgical reform, but the activities are not fully thought out, and are carried through with too much speed and superficiality. The point is not to cast negative judgments on initial attempts but to underline the kinds of organiza-tional capacities that the Church possesses, should it choose to follow through on some of these critical tasks of helping to bring about a cultural mutation.

Control Points in the Church's Participation in the Cultural Mutation Process

When we turn from the potential capacities of the Church for facili-tating a cultural mutation to the actual situation, a number of major problems are quickly apparent: Where does this "new leadership" come from? How are the indigenous idea men to be recruited? How is the organizational cohesion necessary for carrying through such plans ob-tained? How can the masses be resocialized if they don't attend mass and worship services? Which bishops stand ready to promote and support local pastors who will take initiatives for resocialization? These questions bear some remarkable similarities to those that may be asked by political scientists about the problems of political development, or by economists upon applying a theoretical model to a weak and undeveloped economy.

There are at least three points in the Church, in addition to those already mentioned, where added momentum can be given to the process of cultural change:

The role of the papal nuncio. Each country in Latin America receives an official representative from the Holy See. This papal official holds a dual status: He is a member of the official diplomatic corps as a rep-resentative of the Vatican, and he is the official representative of papal policy to the bishops of the national Church. He serves, in this latter capacity, as a center of communication between local bishops and the Holy See, performs innumerable ceremonial roles in relation to the in-stallation of new bishops and the organization of new jurisdictional units, and helps in the selection of bishops for appointments to new or vacant sees. In short, the papal nuncio holds a critical role in the major decisions in a national Church.

It is obvious that this role places a heavy responsibility on the nuncio for shaping the Church, especially at the episcopal level. If the "right kind" of bishops are to be appointed, then the nuncio should also be the "right kind" of man. In turn, the appointment of the nuncios by the pope means that it is he, the pope, who is principally responsible for how a Church is reshaped, particularly at those points where sees are being created or vacated.

The role of the seminaries. The training grounds for future priests are the major seminaries. The curricula they follow and the types of pastoral education provided hold a central impact on the final product. There is, however, good reason to believe that the major seminaries throughout Latin America are strongholds of tradition, or at the very least relatively ineffective centers of theological and pastoral training. Who controls the seminaries? In most instances they are under the direct control of the local bishop, or in the hands of particular religious orders who have the support of the bishop. This means that the bishop, once again, becomes a critical factor in the total formula of building a progressive Church. In turn, it is the nuncio, and ultimately the pope, who assumes the final role in decisions about bishops. But these actors are only part of the total picture, for it is necessary to consider the role that local conditions of an economic, political, or religious nature play in the creation and stimulation of progressive bishops.

The matching of progressive bishops to progressive dioceses. In the course of a recent study that I am completing on twelve dioceses in France, Chile, and the United States, it has become increasingly clear that a progressive bishop does not necessarily make for a progressive diocese and that, in some instances, there can be progressively oriented and developing dioceses without progressive episcopal leadership. The conditions that make for one configuration as against another are in part internal, i.e., the size and complexity of the diocese, the outlook and leadership style of the bishop, etc.[22] But many of the key determinants are situational: the political, economic, demographic, ecological, and religious aspects of the surrounding society. In instances where political and religious competition are keen and where economic growth and mobility (social and territorial) are occurring, the chances are that the general tone and emphasis of the diocese—in terms of lay orientations, pastoral leadership, relations with non-Catholics, etc.—will be progressive, whatever the ideological and leadership tendencies of the bishop. Thus,

[22] These relationships are examined at length in Ivan Vallier, "Comparative Studies of Roman Catholicism: Dioceses as Strategic Units," *Social Compass,* in press.

the allocation of progressive bishops to inherently conservative contexts interrupts the over-all process of change.

The Short Circuiting of the Cultural Role into Politics

Developmental sequences, like electrical currents, can be short circuited. Initiatives are begun or a direction is set; but goals lose meaning, or procedures for taking advantage of the first achievements are diluted, lost, or become available for other efforts. There is a loss of momentum; even more unfortunate, a diversion of mobilizable resources into roles that are inhibitive of the full realization of the sequence.

This short circuiting of the "new Church's religious capital" or its mobilizable resources—motivational, institutional, cultural—can easily take place. I shall briefly describe some of the conditions (external to the Church, and internal) that can help break this momentum.

The process of joining the cultural to the motivational level is central. A Church that moves, in a situation of rapid social change, from an encapsulated position within the conservative block to a more autonomous, charismatic position on the side of social change, adds considerably to the total leverage for social reform and national development. As the Church's top leaders gain a symbolic role in the wider change situation and become associated with the forces that support it, moral authority on behalf of human problems is achieved, rather than moral defensiveness against the solution of such problems. In doing this, the leaders gain a new cultural autonomy and major increments of prestige, visibility, and respect.

But the gains at the cultural level are only part of the total picture. Once that level has been reached, the identification with it is secured, the Church has the possibility (or the responsibility) to initiate other lines of specialized activity having to do with the transformation of motivations and the definition of roles that can integrate those religiously related motivations to specialized developmental tasks.

This crucial juncture is subject to many unwieldy complications or problems. First, religious meanings are necessarily stated in very general terms—secular involvement, servanthood, social justice, etc. These general concepts and the symbols by which they are carried can be related to many types of concrete activities and roles. But if left to themselves, or shifted directly to the political side, they soon lose their generality, and thus one of their principal sources of cultural charisma. Second, the distinction between moving from the cultural meanings to social action or role participation and that of sponsoring a political program is of the utmost importance. It is seemingly logical to move from these meanings to direct political action or to some kind of limited solidarity (small Christian communities); however, there is a crucial intermediary step that has to be taken into account—namely, the working out of generalized action roles that can be modified, according to context and climate, to the exigencies of social change.

SUMMARY

Organized religious systems, under contemporary conditions, inevitably lose traditional sources of support. More important, the officials discover through various appraisals of the situation that the supports remaining are not productive and capable of yielding effective departure points for creating new bases of visibility, influence, and control. But unlike traditional economic and political systems, which can be evaluated according to empirical standards, religious systems tend to graft, supplement, and elaborate "new" roles and action models onto the old in their efforts to overcome the collective anxiety stemming from such factors as loss and deprivation. This gives rise to a series of tensions within the religious system that inevitably spill over into the wider situation and affect the course of change, group conflict, etc. This means that the analysis of "the role of religion in modernization" requires attention to the "strategies," "conflicts," divisions, and "initiatives" that are bred by the religious elites' attempts to build new bases of influence and prestige. The basic outputs and repercussions are not fully addressed by limiting study to the direct or indirect effects of a belief system for variables in the economic, political, and social realms.

A "modernizing" Church, in my theory, is one that develops along multiple dimensions—cultural, bureaucratic, communal, and technical— and in ways that provide the religious system with new bases of influence and visibility which, in turn, enhance, reinforce, and otherwise give positive outputs (or at least neutralize those that deter modernization in the wider society) to spheres in the total society that are crucial to institutional change.

I believe that this dual perspective is critical for formulating theories about the role of religion in modernization, encompassing as it does processes that augment simultaneously the influence of the Church (or at least provide it with new sources of rewards and recognition), and secular processes connected with the process of change in the wider society. Too often, the focus is limited to the beliefs of the religion and their motivational implications, which, in turn, are then correlated with, related to causally, or analyzed through latent function paradigms, in the economic, political, and social spheres.

But, I am suggesting that an organized religious system is a major actor and that its officials have goals, have privileges to protect, have investments in the system, have a sense of obligation to perpetuate their beliefs, etc. These attributes of the religion as an organized interest group imply that the dynamics associated with the pursuits of those interests have to be taken into account when the problem of the role of religion in modernization is approached.

If the officials are united against change or are predisposed to fight for a certain type of traditional monopoly or special privileges, then the religious organization quickly enough becomes either a part of the conservative political-economic sector or a wider part of the class struggle. It becomes a political issue. On the other hand, if there is an opening to society and change and attempts to work with it or ahead of it, it may be that the Church begins to polarize itself and ultimately begins to lose the very kind of symbolic solidarity that is crucial for legitimating change.

The Church's gradual disengagement from direct politics, and its corresponding re-entry into society as a creator of collective symbols that promote a positive meaning of social change, calls attention to only one set of processes that bear on modernization. Motivational change, involving religious identities, conceptions of the religious role, and members' relations to secular society, is equally important. Unless the Church's cultural leadership is supplemented by attitudinal and behavioral change at the grassroots level, the "new Catholicism" remains little more than a competing ideology.[1] This chapter is a description of the motivational problems facing the Church, the kinds of roles gaining visibility among the laity, and a tentative assessment of their significance for both the development of the Church and the modernization of society.

THE CHURCH'S MOTIVATIONAL PROBLEM

In my description of the traditional Church and its established modes of mustering influence, I indicated that diffuse loyalty, religious sentiment, and sacramental conformity

[1] The ideological role of religion is not unimportant; however, it is only one aspect of a wider set of considerations. For particular analyses of religion and ideology, see David E. Apter, "Political Religion in the New Nations, in *Old Societies and New States,* ed. Clifford Geertz (New York: The Free Press, 1963), pp. 57-104; Anthony F. C. Wallace, *Religion, an Anthropological View* (New York: Random House, Inc., 1966), pp. 126-38; Donald Eugene Smith, *Religion and Politics in Burma* (Princeton, N.J.: Princeton University Press, 1965), pp. 117-39.

CHAPTER SIX

The New Church and Motivational Change

among the laity constitute the basic motivational resources available to officials. Although other types of religious involvements are characteristic of baptized Catholics, many of these are tied to devotional activities and group rituals that are centered outside the formal boundaries of the Church. None of the traditional reservoirs of religious motivation is functional for the roles that progressive elites are now defining for Catholicism.

Parallel Structures as a Substitute for a Vigorous Faith

One of the Church's established strategies for protecting the members from secular influences consists in the creation and sponsorship of Catholic charities, Catholic schools, Catholic trade unions, Catholic youth organizations, and sometimes Catholic political parties. These parallel structures help to keep laymen close to the Church even while fulfilling obligations in secular society.[2] Catholic structures follow members into all their major role systems and provide insulating barriers between them and the world. The sociological significance of these elaborate confessional networks is at least twofold: They reduce the possibilities for the integration of Catholics into society, and they indicate that the Church is not willing to trust the layman to be on his own. This suggests that an inverse correlation exists between the elaborateness of confessional structures and the strength of the laity's religious commitments.

This confessional strategy is relatively well institutionalized in most Latin American societies,[3] but less so than in countries like France, Italy, Spain, and Germany.[4] Gradually, however, Catholic strategists are shifting ground and attempting to do away with confessional insulative mechanisms. The present focus in many programs is on a development of motivations that fuse religious and ethical principles with secular roles according to varying contexts. This places a special responsibility on the individual Catholic and, in turn, opens the door for the emergence of autonomous, idiosyncratic, or even charismatic expressions. The very fact that the Church is attempting to reduce its structural involvement in society, i.e., through the jettisoning of confessional structures and clerical

---

[2] Confessional structures are premised on an assumption that the member will lose his faith if allowed to enter fully into the secular world. Religious control is centered in formal organizations, headed by either priests or "lay clerics," i.e., faithful members who have completely internalized the ecclesiastical principles of leadership and obedience.

[3] For a listing of the major confessional organizations, see Carlos Alfaro, *Guía Apostólica Latinoamericana* (Barcelona: Editorial Herder, 1965).

[4] The wide-ranging and extensive patterns of confessional structures in the French Church are described and compared by William Bosworth, *Catholicism and Crisis in Modern France* (Princeton, N.J.: Princeton University Press, 1962).

involvements, means that the insulating, protective mechanisms that have earlier restrained the layman as well as modulated his contacts with society, are no longer viewed as essential. The emphasis is now on open boundaries vis-à-vis the world and a corresponding heightened interest in relating the Church to that world. This is prompting Church elites to search for a new type of layman—one who is integrally involved in religious activities, but also fully involved in secular society.[5]

But the possibilities for creating this Catholic-secular layman are considerably hampered by established features and policies of the Church. For one thing, the Church has very few meaningful rewards to distribute to laymen as means of drawing them into more responsibility. The main mobility line is blocked by the requirements for priesthood. Laymen are prohibited from performing the sacrament of mass, which closes off the possibility for joining lay leadership with central symbolic roles. On another level, the Church is typically fearful of the psychological concomitants of deep religious experiences, such as regenerative conversions. Throughout the centuries it has tried to contain emotion and to reduce the opportunities for the rise of lay charisma. Yet in its present statements and calls to the layman, the Church recognizes the "gifts" or charisms of each person.[6] Every member of the people of God has special gifts and these are to have full expression in the Church. But this formal acknowledgment of the laity's charisms is not a blanket permission for the free expression of religious impulse. The layman's gifts are to be applied to further the work of the Church in the world, rather than to challenge the religious authority of its officials.

Finally, symbolic rewards have lost a good deal of their meaning. The promise of heaven, or the fear of hell, is an effective basis of sanctioning people who have been taught to view the mundane world as unimportant or something that must be temporarily tolerated. But when religious elites begin to invest the world with sacred meaning and make it a primary arena of religious action, supernatural rewards are pushed further into the background. Those who strive to live up to the teachings of the Church are not only obligated to pursue the normal schedule of ritual

[5] These new norms for the action of laymen are delineated in several recent works: "Decree on the Apostolate of the Laity," in *The Documents of Vatican II*, ed. Walter M. Abbott, trans. ed. Joseph Gallagher (New York: Guild Press, 1966), pp. 489-521; Jan Grootaers, "Structures and Living Communities in the Conciliar Church," *Information Documentation on the Conciliar Church* (IDO-C), (Rome, Doss. 67-15/16, May 14, 1967); and Louis J. Putz, "The Layman in Seminary Education," in *Seminary Education in a Time of Change*, eds. James Michael Lee and Louis J. Putz (Notre Dame, Ind.: Fides Publishers, Inc., 1965), pp. 512-19.

[6] This theme is developed in the "Dogmatic Constitution on the Church," in Abbott, ed., *The Documents of Vatican II*, Arts. 30-38, pp. 56-65.

activities and to practice charity but also to help rectify the human situation and bring it into alignment with ethical principles. This redefinition of the situation tends to bring the leadership and procedures of the official Church under empirical scrutiny, since a Church that espouses a goal of offering "service" to the world opens itself to criticism if it fails to carry out this sacred mission. Church organization emerges as an instrument of action, rather than an eternal, sacred embodiment of Christ.[7] Priests and bishops are no longer privileged, unassailable ecclesiastical monarchs but members of the people of God and collaborators in the mission of servanthood. All these themes emanating from Vatican II have helped to shift the phenomenological climate within the Church.

The motivational problem of the Church, as it faces the rank and file, is extremely problematic: it wants more commitment from them, but has few rewards to offer; it wants laymen to be fully in the world, yet also fully integrated in the Church; it wants enthusiasm and a display of initiative, yet is fearful of fomenting religious experiences that may challenge established bases of authority. I shall describe briefly the initiatives being taken by the official Church to make its way through these ambiguities and contradictions, turning then to the pattern of motivations that are emerging more spontaneously among the laymen.

OFFICIAL ATTEMPTS TO RESOCIALIZE THE LAYMAN

To the Church's usual emphases on the cathechism, clerically supervised youth movements, and traditional forms of Catholic Action, other types of adult-centered programs of training, revival, and indoctrination are being added. Some of these are products of Vatican II, such as the study renewal groups that are springing up in the parishes. Others are local modifications of world-wide programs, for example *los Cursillos*. Special revival-type campaigns are also organized in major urban areas. All these, in one way or another, are directed toward enlivening the laity's commitments and mobilizing them for religious action in the world. The Vatican II renewal groups and the specialized work of *los Cursillos* bear special mention.

Renewal Groups in the Parish

These study and training groups are organized under the supervision of the local pastor. Parishioners meet in small groups, usually on a biweekly schedule, to discuss the Bible or basic documents from Vatican II.

---

[7] Some parallel processes in Islam are suggested by Clifford Geertz, *Islam Observed: Religious Development in Morocco and Indonesia* (New Haven: Yale University Press, 1968), pp. 60-62.

In some cases, laymen assume full responsibility for leadership, with no priest in attendance. Norms of equality and open communication are emphasized. Membership is voluntary and leadership responsibility is rotated. Men and women meet together and outsiders (non-Catholics) are usually welcomed. The principal objectives of these meetings are to bring the laity up to date on the Church's teachings, to foster a sense of religious community, and to encourage laymen to integrate the ethical principles of Christianity to their secular activities. The local pastor is one of the most important factors in the development of these groups. The younger, more progressive priests who are often assigned to parishes in growing population areas are reported to be especially interested in promoting these groups.

The "Little Courses in Christianity" (Los Cursillos)

During the past ten years, a new movement of Catholic training for laymen has emerged at various places throughout Latin America. The name of this movement is *Los Cursillos de Cristianidad* or "the little courses in Christianity." [8] The movement originated in the late 1940s in Spain and has since spread to parts of Europe and the Americas. Its aims are at least two: (1) to revive and deepen the laity's allegiances to the Church, and (2) to motivate laymen to engage in apostolic tasks. The strategy is "concentrated revivalism"; the purpose is a "reconversion of apathetic members into apostolic militants."

The *cursillos* gain legitimation to operate in a given diocese through approval by the bishop. Some bishops are against them and prevent their activities; others accept them or support them; finally, some attempt to coopt the Cursillista leaders and to use the courses in special ways to bring about pastoral renewel.

The central procedure of the *cursillos* is the organization of three-day "retreats" for adult males or females (not together), during which time an intense program of special lectures, meditation sessions, small-group discussions, and testimonies of faith is carried out. Laymen are selected for a given retreat by the local pastor and moved to some isolated premise for the duration of the courses. Spiritual exercises, reportedly bearing some resemblance to those developed by St. Ignatius Loyola, the founder of the Society of Jesus (1540), are followed. Laymen frequently undergo a basic reorientation to the principles of faith, to themselves, and to

[8] The basic goals and features of *los Cursillos* are described in Juan Hervas, *Leaders' Manual for Cursillos in Christianity*, authorized Eng. trans. of the 4th Spanish ed., Collin H. Portnoff, *et al.* (Phoenix, Ariz.: Ultreya Press, 1964). For a recent report on the growth of the *Cursillos* in Argentina, see "Tucumán, reino del cursillismo," *Primera Plana* (Buenos Aires), Año VII, No. 319, February 10, 1969, pp. 60-63.

others. In short, a fundamental type of conversion often occurs, generating a great deal of self-analysis, emotional expression, and renewed dedication to Catholicism. This generalized motivation, in turn, is intended to serve as a basic spiritual resource for Church organizations that specialize in apostolic work.

It is relatively clear that these courses arouse interests and emotions that are deeply confessional and thereby traditional. Furthermore, the integration of the *cursillos* with other apostolic organizations, such as Catholic Action, the Legion of Mary, or the Society of St. Vincent de Paul, is extremely weak. Laymen who pass through the courses are thereby stimulated toward "some kind of meaningful action," but often find it hard to "connect up" with already established organizations. There are several typical consequences: (1) a rapid diminishing of the original impulses and interests; (2) a heightened activism that easily becomes turned into confessional militancy; (3) a primitive attachment to other Cursillistas as a means of trying to relive and perpetuate the original experience; (4) high degrees of anomie and frustration in the post training period regarding the nature of the task that is to be carried out.

The work of the *cursillos,* and the success (in terms of interest and experiences) they have achieved in some places, is demonstrating to Church leaders that laymen are searching for emotional opportunities that are not available in the normal life of the parish. Although critics of the *cursillos* view them as stimulants to fanaticism and personal confusion, it is difficult to avoid the conclusion that these courses tap a deep undercurrent of psychological need. The problem, at least for the progressive leaders, is how to use the technique of the *cursillos* without fostering traditional commitments, or how to bring about member conversions that are not "fundamentalistic" in nature. Modified uses of the *cursillos* in certain dioceses indicate that this dual goal is achievable. When laymen are assigned to the retreats, greater emphasis is placed on the teachings of Vatican II, and the participants are given subsequent responsibilities in parish renewal and study groups. It is not unlikely that the basic mechanisms of the *cursillos* will be increasingly adapted to facilitate progressive goals and basic programs of parish reform.

The renewal groups and the *cursillos* are recent additions to the Church's elaborate system of Catholic Action movements, family programs (Christian Family movement), leadership conferences, and rural training centers. Each of the newer emphases is distinct in format and purposes, yet both embody techniques that stress "human relations" principles of group activity: indirect leadership, open communication, problem-solving assignments, psychological phasing, and decentralized decision making. Coeducational membership is also gaining significance, as in the renewal groups. Gradually the Church is recognizing that traditional methods of training, consisting of direct indoctrination, rational presentations of ideas, and formal styles of authority, do not produce either religious commitment or social responsibility. More important, there is an increasing awareness among churchmen that laymen who have assumed responsibility in the internal activities of the Church (leadership roles, participation in group development, etc.) are also those who are most inclined to enter fully into secular society without a lot of confessional preoccupations.

In short, depth involvements within the Church generate an internalization of religious norms, making it possible for the layman to achieve flexible, autonomous adaptations in secular roles. The overhead of confessional structures is replaced by a laity that has roots in the Church, through a specialized role, but correspondingly holds full commitments to secular activities. This pattern begins to approach the type of religious role that is found in countries characterized by denominational pluralism: Individuals routinely engage in specialized forms of religious activity, according to their own choice, yet maintain a fully integrated relationship to society. In place of attempts by the religious institutions to provide the rules for secular roles, or to insulate the membership from outside influences, there is concentration by leaders on developing the local Church as a center for religious advice and social expression, ultimately to "turn the laymen loose" to make their own way.

THE LAITY'S FELT NEEDS: EMERGING DEMANDS FROM BELOW [9]

The efforts of Catholic elites to reshape the motivations of the laity are typically unattuned to the latter's conceptions of priorities and needs. Elites generally begin with some conception of the Church's adaptive problem and then try to mobilize motivations as part of a designated solution. In some instances, the aspirations and felt needs of the laity are not known; in other instances, they may be known but ignored. But as the Church loses its capacity to command obedience and passes into a phase where it must rely on voluntary compliance, the feelings of the rank and file assume a new importance. This observation takes on even greater significance in the present period, since the laity is now being defined as the chief linkage between Church and world.

[9] Materials of this section are based primarily on field interviews carried out by Rocco Caporale with laymen in four dioceses in Chile in 1966 as part of my comparative project on the change in the Church in France, Chile, and the United States. This study is sponsored and financed by the Institute of International Studies, University of California, Berkeley.

The documents and emphases of Vatican II directly and indirectly encouraged laymen to make themselves heard in the Church. Bishops and priests are admonished to consider the needs of the laity and to bring the rank and file into relationships of consultation and collaboration. In many dioceses and parishes throughout the world, these norms are being institutionalized. Laymen are gaining participative roles in ritual activities and administrative work. Priests are asking them for suggestions and help. Some bishops have established consultative forums and planning bodies that bear on pastoral work. Yet in the majority of instances, the pace is very slow, token rather than authentic arrangements are established, and the age-long distance between officials and the rank and file is undiminished.

The picture in Latin America varies. A small minority of bishops and priests have heeded the counsels of Vatican II and are proceeding to initiate structural reforms. However, a number of complex problems emerge in the wake of these efforts: The progressive policies of bishops are thwarted by local pastors, the sheer size of the parishes diminishes the possibilities for personal leadership and two-way communication, personal ambitions destroy incipient group developments, too many projects are begun and left unfinished, and, of no small importance, many laymen show a marked reluctance to "get involved." There are, then, some new initiatives from the top, a great deal of movement and motion, and a few prospective lines of solid reform. Concurrently, however, a whole new upsurge of rising aspirations and rank-and-file unrest is evident. In the midst of this flux and ferment, a number of motivational tendencies and explicit demands are observable. I shall identify the emerging patterns that bear centrally on the general problem of motivational change.

Demands for Power

Many laymen are asking for a share in the governing of the Church and stand in protest against prevailing patterns of authority and leadership. Officials are charged with administrative incompetence, misuse of authority, wasteful allocations of money, and calculated indifference to the capacities of laymen. These indictments do not imply imminent elimination of religious offices, nor the development of a full democracy. Instead they indicate an interest in an upgrading of leadership effectiveness; and it is in that context that laymen feel they have a right to take over some of the responsibilities, especially those that have to do with the temporal administration of the Church.

The sociological principle at stake is that of structural differentiation which, in the Church system, would separate the domain of religious authority from the domains of routine administration and program development. Laymen do not want to be bishops or priests, i.e., spiritual authorities. Their demands are for opportunities to assume responsibility for some of the tasks that, at present, are being carried out ineffectively, and that appear to keep churchmen from developing their roles as spiritual authorities.

Demands for Communal Solidarity

On quite a different analytical plane, laymen are pressing for structural changes that will open the way for more intense and more meaningful forms of socioritual activity. Typical themes are "solidarity," "familialism," "community," and "spiritual depth." The traditional parish is viewed as completely outmoded, both as a concept and as a concrete arrangement. Its territorial definition, its typically enormous size (both geographically and in terms of constituency), its overemphasis on formal sacramentalism, and the way it defines the role of the priest, add up, in the minds of many laymen, to an institutional zero. Some of these issues are being diminished in their sharpness by the growth of the parish-based renewal groups, mentioned above. But, on the whole, these official initiatives are viewed as insufficient. Hence laymen, with the support of some priests, are taking the initiative to realize new forms of socioritual activity. These "underground" groups favor the "house mass," the communal meal that is centered around communion under both species (wafer and wine), group confession, spontaneous and *ad hoc* forms of liturgical activity, equality between priest and layman (except for the priest's special role as celebrant), and an intimate social fellowship. Meetings usually take place biweekly or monthly, with roughly twenty to twenty-five members in attendance. The size of the group is kept small in order to enhance the possibilities for primary group relations.

The motivations that underlie this emerging style of socioritual activity are undoubtedly mixed, including both anxieties over isolation and a need to be part of an elite movement. But the sociological significance is readily apparent: As the extended kinship pattern and the natural community associated with residential life grow weaker, people turn more directly to the Church for solidarity and fellowship. These needs are stimulated further by the emphasis of recent Church teachings on the value of religious community and member-to-member solidarity. All the theological themes that touch on these horizontal dimensions of Church life—"people of God," the liturgical community," "pastoral ministry," and "congregational harmony"—find their most vigorous expression in these socioritual cells. I do not intend to convey the impression that these activities are sweeping the Latin American Church. The most that can be said is that these aspirations are increasingly apparent among the rank and file, and some initiatives of a quasi-clandestine nature are being taken to realize them.

Demands for Organizational Autonomy in Relation to Sociopolitical Issues

A third cluster of demands vis-à-vis the official Church is emerging among Catholics whose interests focus on action in the world and who want to help solve human problems in society as part of their religious involvements. These laymen want to shift the Church's prestige and influence to the side of those forces that are trying to eradicate traditional structures, bring about revolutionary change, and build the "good society." The main sponsorship for this line of action comes from university students, young professionals, and some priests who have held important leadership roles in movements of Catholic Action. The main rub comes from the fact that these groups are, intentionally or unintentionally, identified as "Catholic" which, automatically, implicates the hierarchy. By the official line, no group or movement that bears a direct relation to the institutional Church can engage in explicit politics. This is why the Christian Democratic parties not only insist on their autonomous status but are also regarded by most Church leaders as "non-Church."

It is in the context of these fine-line distinctions that the more politically oriented movements of laymen are asking for complete autonomy to pursue their "religious objectives." However, they have not yet solved the problems of financial autonomy, nor do they show a complete willingness to go fully secular; therefore they generate considerable amounts of tension both within the Church and in the wider society.

The ideal state of affairs for these laymen is Church support but complete autonomy to set their own goals, strategies, and activities. The ideal solution for the Church, it appears, would be for laymen to drop their collective identification with "things Catholic" and proceed, as individual citizens, to enter politics along lines of their own choosing. Some gains toward the solution of these opposing clusters of interests are made in situations where a strong, reformist Christian Democratic party exists. Laymen who want to move directly into political action, within a framework of Christian thinking, can find a place in such a party, as many laymen did over the past few years in Chile. But some laymen want to go beyond the Christian Democratic position, even in Chile. They opt for a more radical, and revolutionary, form of politics, thus defining the centrist-reform orientations of Christian Democracy as essentially conservative. Needless to say, their claims have an undeniable validity within the emerging framework of Church thought.

Post-Vatican emphases on the role of the Church in accelerating social justice, solving human problems, and erasing repressive structures are now part of the theological and ideological climate. Radical laymen can point to these ideas as legitimate departure points for action. Their demands for autonomy, within a wider Christian framework, represent one of the major dilemmas of the contemporary Church. If it supports those demands, it stands to be readily implicated in politics of the left which, in turn, prompts rightist-reactionary responses from traditional officials and laymen. On the other hand, if it jettisons the revolutionaries in order to preserve its "nonpolitical" policy, it becomes implicitly associated with the status quo and, additionally, loses a sector of its most forward-looking laity.

These three motivational emergents—demands for power, demands for religious community, and demands for organizational autonomy—are indications of felt needs among an increasing number of Catholic laymen in Latin America, as well as in many other places throughout the Western world. These demands and aspirations flow from the life situations of many laymen and appear to represent the bases for bargaining with their hierarchical superiors. Although they do not articulate it in the terms that a sociologist would use, laymen are implying that the norms that officials are setting for them will not be taken seriously unless they get some of the things they want. On another level, it is clear that the more the official Church finds ways of meeting some of these demands, the more it will find that it has a laity that is capable of both "being in the Church and being in the world." The kinds of involvements and experiences that laymen are asking for cannot help but bind them more deeply into the religious life of the Church while, at the same time, increasing their freedom to find their own way in the world. It is in this context that the emerging pastoral-congregational strategy in the local church bears special mention.

THE INCIPIENT CONGREGATIONAL PATTERN

Many nominal Catholics will continue to move away from the institutional Church and take on completely secular values. An equally important segment of the laity on the other end of the attitudinal spectrum will assume more entrenched, conservative postures toward the faith, and mount successive campaigns against the progressive forces in the Church. Between these two inclinations, however, a large middle sector is staying in the Church and moving with it in its hesitant pattern of change. At this point, the main direction of this middle sector is not clear, and many of its elites evidence confusions about priorities and the choice of means for implementing goals. Some progressive elites want to move directly into politics, make the Church a major organized force for radical change, and leave the conservatives to their favorite preoccupations. Other elites opt for a moderate, but progressive stance that facilitates socioeconomic change and simultaneously carries through moderate structural reforms within the Church.

A third group of progressives, who currently represent only a small minority, are beginning to recognize that a "modern Church" or a progressive Catholicism depends significantly on the development of a more specialized religious strategy wherein the efforts of the leaders are focused on creating religious symbols, providing pastoral leadership, encouraging new forms of spiritual expression, and injecting new degrees of flexibility into the local Church. This emerging model, hinted at in earlier sections, endorses at least two sociological principles. First, it defines the priest's role as a spiritual leader within the local Church, as against a clerical authority in society; second, it defines the main function of the local Church as a socioreligious community from which laymen proceed into society as autonomous Christians. For want of a better term I shall refer to this as the pastoral-congregational model.[10]

The stimulants to this pastoral-congregational emphasis come, in part, from the theological emphases of Vatican II. Equally important is the growing visibility and influence of the Protestant churches and their flexible procedures for establishing new congregations, organizing worship, involving laymen, and encouraging voluntarism. Although progressive Catholics are not willing to grant the Protestants a completely equal place with Roman Catholicism as authentic carriers of the true faith, they are becoming increasingly open to some of the structural principles Protestantism emphasizes. These two stimulants, along with the emerging felt needs of the laity for more vigorous forms of local Church life mentioned above, are helping to give the pastoral-congregational model a viable place in the wider armatorium of change strategies.

Of course, the implied change of leadership role for the clergy and the corresponding change in the definition of the layman's role are not easily achieved. Latin American priests are accustomed to the rewards that come with a diffuse position of public authority. Having played the part

---

[10] The "new pastors" who are helping to focus and facilitate this congregational pattern are described in Ivan Vallier, "Religious Elites: Differentiations and Developments in Roman Catholicism," in *Elites in Latin America*, eds. Seymour Martin Lipset and Aldo Solari (New York: Oxford University Press, Inc., 1967), pp. 205-9. A more specific report on the efforts of pastorally oriented priests in Chile is provided by Thomas G. Sanders, "The Priests of the People," Field Report to the Institute of Current World Affairs, New York, N.Y., TGS-11, March 24, 1968.

of community leader, political adviser, and primary educator,[11] all of which provide diffuse influence in society, it is somewhat difficult to move back into the Church and limit activities to spiritual and pastoral activities. Similarly, the layman, accustomed to the concept of a Catholic society and reared on the idea that the Church should play an organized role in secular affairs, has become especially dependent on its protective and supervisory functions. Moreover, the layman has tended to make his Catholic status an integral part of his major secular roles, instead of defining it as a differentiated and specialized segment of his total involvements. The difference between a layman who assumes a Catholic society, and thereby fuses his religious status with secular involvements, and a Catholic who assumes a secular society but holds a specialized membership and involvement in the Church as a religious system, is extraordinarily subtle but of major sociological significance.

The main mechanism that operates to lift the clergy out of society and correspondingly helps to differentiate the member's Catholic status from secular statuses is a local Church that combines a religious-social program with voluntarism, lay participation, and pastoral leadership. These features, in turn, gain significance and meaning to the degree that the members of the local Church represent a common class position. Communal attachments and psychological identifications with the group are fostered among people who share a class or status position. The traditional, territorial parish, on the other hand, typically encompasses diverse occupational and status groups. Members who share ritual premises do not generally share a sufficient number of social statuses to provide a basis for communal identity. In turn, the traditional liturgical style of ritual formalism and individual response in the traditional parish precludes the possibility for an emergence of horizontal involvements. Pastoral preaching, which often functions to give religious services a collective meaning, is not typically emphasized, again decreasing the chances that parishioners would experience a sense of social togetherness.

The central feature of the congregational trend is personal, religious leadership in the local Church. The primary goals are to teach the gospel, to bring meaning to ritual activities in light of these teachings and the secular situation, and to promote social fellowship and religious community. The standards for combining these elements into a leadership style are fluid and changing. In one setting the pastor's emphasis may be on relating traditional devotional interests to the framework of Christian ethics; in other places, the stress may be placed on the role of the sacra-

[11] These aspects of the priest's role in rural Colombia are dealt with extensively by Gustavo Jiménez Cadena, *Sacerdote y Cambio Social* (Bogotá: Ediciones Tercer Mundo, 1967).

ments in the shaping of the religious community. Where one pastor may emphasize personal contact with people in the local area without pressing them to increase their sacramental diligence, another may work personally with family groups and school-age children. The pastoral strategy tends to be both outer directed, in the sense of attuning religious leadership to contemporary trends, and inner directed, whereby the basic rituals and preaching function are defined as springboards for bringing religious meaning and communal dimensions to scheduled services.

The fact that the priest who adopts a pastoral policy extends the scope of his religious leadership within the Church, i.e., going beyond the role of ritual leader, means that his possibilities for collaboration with the laity are increased. Opportunities for laymen to share in leadership tend, in turn, to increase their interest in the local Church and, therefore, the possibilities that each person will be able to integrate social and religious norms. Along other lines, the pastoral emphasis modulates the laymen's protests against hierarchy, formality, and impersonal structures, since the rank and file are provided participative and leadership responsibilities. Finally, the growth of communal solidarity within the Church gives depth to the religious role. When this occurs, the laymen find it possible to be in the Church, through a specialized role, and in the world, without having to rely on the traditional insulating mechanisms and official initiatives.

The significance of these emerging congregational patterns for the redefinition of the Catholic's relationship to society is at least twofold. (1) The fusion of social and religious identities in close-knit associational groupings concentrates a wide range of the layman's loyalties to a single membership role. If this occurs, the Catholic status is more fully differentiated from secular statuses. Moreover, the expressive and participative opportunities that are built into these groups probably deepen his religious feelings and his attachments to Christian norms without obliging him to represent the Church in society. The congregational formats thus bring about a greater specialization in the religious role, and give it a depth that is sustained in everyday encounters. (2) The layman, in acquiring a sense of Christianity as an ethical religion, begins to shift his notion of the criteria for being a good Catholic from that of sacramental participation and defense of the institutional Church to one that relates religious principles to all roles. The socialization that takes place in the newer groups strengthens the principal aspects of religious action over and above proscriptions, prescriptions, and detailed rules.

This twofold process—a deepening and narrowing of the religious membership role and a transferring of ethical responsibility to the person—helps to foster a new type of secular role. This role is distinguished by a normative orientation to the socioethical principles of Christianity which, at one level, gives all aspects of society religious significance and, at the individual level, assigns each member a responsibility to relate those norms to his major roles and social relationships.

The pastoral trend is only beginning to gain a competitive position in Latin American societies. Its chances for rapid development are relatively poor. Most of the clergy are tied to traditional styles of leadership and view the laity with ambivalence. Moreover, the fact that the typical parish is extensive in geographical size and comprehensive of thousands of members means that there are few structural conditions for the development of the small, congregational style. The restoration of the diaconate, as a halfway house between the laity and the priest, may prove to be an important factor in the development of the pastoral format. But since the deacon is not permitted to celebrate mass, his role is robbed of one of the most important mechanisms for tying social needs to ritual activity.

Despite these problems, it is increasingly clear that some kind of congregational voluntarism is emerging, and the more rapidly it gains solid institutional support, the higher the possibilities that the Catholic masses will begin to value full participation in secular society. Unless the traditional conceptions of the Catholic's role are abandoned, there is little likelihood that the efforts of the theologians and ethical prophets will become important forces on behalf of modernization. Both levels of development are crucial—the further institutionalization of the clergy's role as socioethical spokesmen, and the further institutionalization of the laity's role as secular Christians. In all this, the role of the local priest is crucial. The local religious leader becomes a central integrating point for these two processes. In turn, it is the local Church and its related associational activities—liturgical, pastoral, and social—that become crucial for both providing the basis for religious community and orienting members to assume fully integrated roles in society.

The modernization of the Church, at the local level and in terms of the average member's roles, takes place to the degree that the locus of religious control becomes transferred to the person, rather than resting either in the institutional Church or the political group. By locus of religious control, I mean the unit of decision making regarding choices among action alternatives.[12] The traditional Church and most of its subsequent extensions (among which I would include the dominant emphases of Vatican II) make the official Church or its official representa-

---

[12] For a related, but more general, analysis of the place of the person in "modern religion," see Robert N. Bellah, "Religious Evolution," *American Sociological Review*, XXIX, No. 3, June, 1964, 371-74.

tives the locus of religious control. In Catholic Action movements, e.g., the chaplain priest is the locus of final decision making (although the exercise of this role may not be necessary since most of the militants are often more "clerical" than the cleric). Similarly, in the Vatican II model, the essential basis of religious control is the "collaborative group" which, inevitably, includes members of the priesthood (even though this control and the decisions may have a wider sociological base, or take place within new kinds of concepts and self-images). On the other hand, in the emerging pastoral emphasis, the locus of religious control is the individual who has experienced the support of the congregation. The outcome, at the level of the person, is an orientation to the world that emphasizes responsibility for reshaping it and affecting it through deliberate action. The layman of this persuasion is not focused on escape from the world through religious conformity and sacramental involvements, nor is he dependent on the priest or clergy as the creator and judge of worldly actions. Instead, he is oriented to a religious culture that is organized around principles of human consequence. This is the chief value referent. Second, this new layman holds a role in the institutional Church by which various types of expressive and social needs are met. Activities in the Church are supportive of involvement in the world.

The positive implications of this model for religious and political development are hard to overestimate. Since it places the member in the world but in tension with a religious culture, he gains a stable set of value referents for choosing principles of action, yet he is not either a representative of the official Church nor oriented to it as a corporate social actor. His religious role is very specialized, and of secondary importance to his activities that have to do with integrated Christian principles with everyday roles, whether social, occupational, or political.

SUMMARY STATEMENT

The reinsertion of the religiously autonomous Church in society is facilitative of social change or modernization to the degree that bishops exercise socioethical leadership and to the degree that laymen—who hold continuous and complete status involvements in the secular world—gain capabilities for integrating their religious and nonreligious roles. As the bishops individually, and—even more important—collectively, assume responsibility for augmenting a culture of change, laymen are confronted with the dual burden of freedom and responsibility. They, rather than the institutional Church, become the basic decision-making unit with respect to choice among alternative courses of action; they, rather than the clergy, are left to integrate religious and secular expectations. In short, the new layman—operating in the world with reference to the general religio-ethical principles articulated by the episcopacy—is a person who has internalized religious authority and religious values, and thus becomes in many ways an autonomous Christian.

Yet the problems that emerge in shaping rank-and-file members for this role in society are characteristically manifold. Laymen are accustomed to a religious role that combines conformity to ritual obligations and idiosyncratic acts of piety and devotion. The responsibility for relating religious norms to social roles has been so far left to Church officials and priests. I have shown, however, that these traditional patterns tie the Church to temporizing, political strategies (with adverse consequences for the development of the political system), and perpetuate types of rank-and-file outlooks and behaviors that tend to retraditionalize secular motivations. Gradually, these configurations are being undercut or eclipsed by organized programs of training and resocialization and, of equal importance, by an emphasis on the social-expressive functions of the local Church. The congregational trend not only provides laymen with roles that help to internalize religious norms, but also fuses rituals, symbols, and class interests into a specialized type of associational activity. As the layman is afforded more opportunities to move deeper into the local Church, he inevitably gains a greater capacity to be a fully secular man.

My discussions thus far have emphasized
types of Catholicism, changing strategies
of influence, and incipient structural
developments without systematic
reference to national situations. This
chapter provides a measure of empirical
balance by comparing five national
Churches—Argentina, Brazil, Chile,
Colombia, and Mexico. The objective of
these comparisons is to identify broad
patterns of variation of normative
and institutional change along lines
that have been formulated in the
evolutionary model presented in Chapter
IV. Three sections divide the chapter.
The first section presents qualitative
profiles of the current situation in
the five national Churches. Section two
formulates four analytical dimensions,
derived from the evolutionary model, as
bases for recording similarities and
variations. In the final section I take
up the problem of explanation and
attempt to isolate the conditions that
stimulate Church development.

PROFILES OF NATIONAL CHURCHES

The national Churches in Latin America
are all parts of a single system of
faith, dogmas, rituals, and authority
structures that distinguishes Roman
Catholicism as a universal religion.
However, these commonalities constitute
only a broad canopy under which
CHAPTER SEVEN   many important sociological variations exist.

Influence Systems and Church
Development: National Variations

Churches not only differ in membership size and in the composition, quantities, and distribution of clergy, but also in organizational configurations.[1] Some churches are totally organized into established dioceses, e.g., Cuba, Argentina, El Salvador, Haiti, and Uruguay. Other Churches, such as Brazil, Peru, and Colombia still embrace significant "missionary territories" that fall under the jurisdiction of the Congregation for the Evangelization of Peoples (formerly the Congregation for the Propagation of the Faith) in Rome. Many variations in formal jurisdictional balance obtain cross-nationally. Churches also differ in terms of the ecological distributions of the membership, i.e., urban-rural differences. More than sixty percent of the population in Uruguay, Argentina, Chile, and Venezuela lives in urban areas, while in Guatemala, Ecuador, Bolivia, Paraguay, and Colombia more than sixty percent of the population lives in the country or in small towns and villages.[2] All of these differences help to give national Churches particular characteristics and styles.

The five national Churches examined here make up a very important sector of the entire Latin American Church. Out of a total of 540 jurisdictional units constituting the Latin American Church in 1965, 364 are comprehended by the Churches of Argentina, Brazil, Chile, Colombia, and Mexico.[3] During the same year, 1965, there were 42,669 priests in Latin America of whom 31,871 held assignments in these five countries.[4] More important for present purposes, the five Churches I have selected are all significant arenas of post-Conciliar ferment and innovation, and thus draw our attention with regard to processes of institutional change. Of course the Church in Cuba holds special significance as both a part of a society that has undergone a recent political revolution and as a reference point for particular groups of Catholics in other Latin American countries. I do not include it here, however, except by indirect reference, because I have not carried out field research in Cuba and I do not choose to rely on the meager reports that describe the Cuban Church's present situation.[5]

[1] Descriptive data on the morphological and demographic features of the Latin American Churches are provided by Isidoro Alonso, *La Iglesia en América Latina,* Fribourg, Switzerland, FERES, 1964; and in *The Priesthood in Latin America* (no author cited), *Pro Mundi Vita* Monographs No. 22, Brussels, Belgium, 1968. For detailed, annual changes consult the *Annuario Pontifico.*

[2] *Statistical Abstract of Latin America, 1965,* Los Angeles, University of California, Latin American Center, 1966, Table 7, p. 14.

[3] Isidoro Alonso, *Estadísticas Religiosas de América Latina,* September, 1966, Table A 3, Mimeo.

[4] These figures are drawn from *The Priesthood in Latin America* (no author cited), *Pro Mundi Vita* Monographs No. 22, Brussels, Belgium, 1968, Table 3, p. 10.

[5] For recent articles on the Cuban Church, see "A Cuba: Fidel Castro Chez le Nonce. La Situation Serait-elle 'Normale,'" *Informations Catholiques Internationales,* No. 303, January 1, 1968, pp. 16-17; "Moment of Truth for the Church in Cuba,"

The Colombian Church

I begin my descriptions with Colombia because its Church, of all the five, possesses the most authentic shapes and styles of traditional Catholicism.[6] The Colombian Church is deeply grounded in the whole institutional life of the society and thus holds higher degrees of ritual, educational, and territorial monopoly than do the Churches in Argentina, Brazil, Chile, and Mexico. Priests are visible, as well as influential, in every sphere of society and correspondingly play key roles as religious authorities, ritual agents, diffuse communal leaders, and members of important secular decision-making groups.[7] Structural interdependencies between the Church and major role systems in society are typical: in education, welfare work, rural development, and social elite circles.

Colombia, as a nation, is segmented geographically and culturally.[8] Although Bogota is the national capital, there are actually seven or eight distinct regional sections, each of which holds its own social identity. These segmental patterns favor the traditional Church's organizational style. Influence can be generated through particularistic relations, *ad hoc* arrangements, and direct action in relation to local events. Laymen are largely "clients"—dormant, loyal members concerned with their ritual obligations and the appropriate sacramental services of the priest. The Colombian Church's orientation to territorial space as an indicator of religious strength is attested to by the efforts it has made to keep competing religious groups out of the country. Most of its leaders are thus concerned with holding operations, not only with respect to the privileges that the

---

CIF Reports (Cuernavaca, Mexico), Vol. V, No. 3, February 1, 1966, 23-24; and Anne Power, "The Church in Cuba," *Commonweal,* Vol. LXXXIX, No. 22, March 7, 1969, 704-5.

[6] Basic historical materials on the Church in Colombia are provided by Antonio de Egaña, *Historia de la Iglesia en la América Española* (Madrid: Biblioteca de Autores Cristianos, 1966), pp. 470-555; J. Lloyd Mecham, *Church and State in Latin America: A History of Politico-Ecclesiastical Relations,* rev. ed. (Chapel Hill: University of North Carolina Press, 1966), Chaper V, "The Religious Problem in the Constitutional History of Colombia," pp. 115-38; Carey Shaw, Jr., "Church and State in Colombia as Observed by American Diplomats, 1834-1906," *The Hispanic American Historical Review,* XXI, No. 4, November, 1941, 577-613; and Gustavo Pérez and Isaac Wust, *La Iglesia en Colombia. Estructuras Eclesiásticas* (Bogotá: FERES, 1962).

[7] The priest's extensive influence in rural Colombian society is indicated in a recent study: Gustavo Jiménez Cadena, *Sacerdote y Cambio Social* (Bogotá: Ediciones Tercer Mundo, 1967).

[8] Consult Everett E. Hagen, *On the Theory of Social Change. How Economic Growth Begins* (Homewood, Ill.: Dorsey Press, 1962), Chapter 15, "The Transition in Colombia," pp. 353-84; T. Lynn Smith, *Colombia: Social Structure and the Process of Development* (Gainesville: University of Florida Press, 1967).

Concordat of 1887 supplies but also in terms of maintaining the physical boundaries of its religious empire.[9]

These are the dominant patterns. Against these, several lines of progressive and more radical activity are being forged. One of these is known as *Acción Cultural Popular* (ACPO) and involves specialized educational programs for the peasants.[10] Its formal aim is to foster change in basic values, agricultural and health practices, and social identities through a network of radio broadcasting centers and local leadership cadres. However religious and moral emphases, corresponding to the more traditional teachings of the Church, are infused into the work of technical and social education. This mixture of the modern and the ecclesiastical appears to reduce the impact of both. Although enormous financial investments and organizational efforts have gone into the program, there are few indications that it is fostering changes in either the *campesinos'* commitments to the Church or in socioeconomic motivations.

Another set of initiatives, more in keeping with the spirit of Vatican II, consists of pastoral reforms, the development of urban community centers, and the establishment of agencies for empirical research, documentation, and the production of educational films. Catholics involved in these enterprises readily identify with a small emerging progressive sector of the episcopate. The emphasis is on change, both in the Church and in society, through specialized organizations, the implementation of themes expressed in recent social encyclicals, and by avoiding political confrontations. These initiatives are not very significant in the context of the whole Church and still lack support from most members of the hierarchy. But the phenomenon that has done most to reduce the visibility of these progressive efforts is the growth of the Christian revolutionaries as a movement of radical protest.

Within the past three years a small number of priests, supported by university students and a mixed contingent of adult laymen, has been attempting to develop a power base of sufficient strength to "break the establishment"—religious and secular. Taking the late Camilo Torres as the martyred hero [11] and Marxist concepts as a basis for their rhetoric, these groups engage in protest demonstrations, rally support against

[9] Gordon H. Van Sickle, "The Background of Protestant Suppression in Colombia," *The Iliff Review*, XI, No. 3, Fall, 1954, 3-20. For a broad description of religion in Colombia, consult B. Haddox, *Religious Institutions of Colombia* (Ph.D. dissertation, University of Florida, 1962).

[10] The *Acción Cultural Popular* program is described by Gustavo Jiménez Cadena, *Sacerdote y Cambio Social: Estudio Sociológico en Los Andes Colombianos*, Bogotá, Colombia, Ediciones Tercer Mundo, 1967, pp. 109-17.

[11] The ideological tenets and aims of this movement in its early stages are stated in "El 'Caso' del Padre Camilo Torres," *Inquietudes*, No. 5, Número Especial, Bogotá, Colombia, Ediciones Tercer Mundo, July 30, 1965.

the hierarchy, and promote a program of radical social justice and of authentic Christian communities. Much of the leadership for this movement comes from members of the Golconda Group.[12] This group of priests (originally fifty in number) has developed a platform of action that includes recourse to violence under certain conditions. In recent months these Christian revolutionaries have gained considerable publicity and appear to some observers to be gaining strength.

There are however certain features of the Colombian situation that reduce the movement's possibilities for achieving noticeable power. The rhetoric of "violence," for example, touches a very sensitive and anxiety-producing theme among the Colombian people. The ravages of terror and violence that have dotted the countryside over the past fifteen years have steeled the populace and most elite groups against any group that begins to preach violence as a political instrument. By indentifying themselves with the phenomenon of violence, the Christian revolutionaries undercut a major portion of their potential legitimation and, as well, repel many of the Catholic progressives who are ready to help promote social change. In short, what could be a rather widespread movement of progressive pressure within the Church is being interrupted by a minority of Catholics who have emerged as symbols of a dreaded political strategy.

The present dynamics of the Colombian Church are focused, then, around the tensions that result from a preponderance of traditional strength, a hesitant progressive sector, and the activities of the rebels or revolutionaries.[13] But the basic trends that have marked the Colombian Church for many years—clerical influence, expansive educational programs, loyal and passive laymen, and close ties between Church and State—continue. It is expected that the Church will try to hold to these patterns through the near future. If turbulence increases, the key leaders

[12] The Golconda Group appears to have gotten underway during the summer of 1968 just prior to the highly publicized and controversial 39th International Eucharistic Congress which met in Bogotá (August 18-25, 1968) and coincident with the appearance of Paul VI's *Humanae Vitae,* July 25, 1968. The fifty priests who make up the nucleus of the Golconda Group met in a remote part of Colombia to develop a charter for accelerating change in the Church and in society. In December, 1968, this group met again to establish a common line of action. The results of the December meeting are available in a formal document entitled "Segundo Encuentro del Grupo Sacerdotal de Golconda: Documento Final," December 13, 1968. A more specific expression of the goals and preferred procedures of the Golconda Group appeared in a speech by Father René García Lizarralde delivered to students at the National University in Bogotá during April, 1969. See James E. Goff, "Father García's Answers to Students' Questions at the National University of Colombia," Bogotá, April 11, 1969, Mimeo, James and Margaret Goff, Bogotá, Colombia, translators and distributors.

[13] Divisions within the Colombian hierarchy are examined briefly in an unauthored report, "L'État de L'Opinion en Amérique Latine à L'Heure de Medellin," *Informations Catholiques Internationales,* No. 319, September 1, 1968, pp. 5-6.

of the established Church will be inclined to seek organized political support or turn to making direct appeals to Catholic sentiment and traditional loyalties. On the other hand, if the revolutionaries decline in importance or turn to more acceptable tactics, the small but growing progressive sector may hold a chance for shifting the Church toward change and development. But in either case, there are few indications that the Colombian Church will move quickly into an advanced stage of development.

The Argentine Church [14]

Whereas the Church in Colombia is typically viewed as combining traditional values with popular forms of religiosity, the Argentine Church has a reputation of "conservatism," i.e., a defensive posture toward modern society, a hesitant public leadership that leads to political ambiguities, and an internal rigidity. These broad characterizations are, of course, stereotypical and somewhat misleading. At the same time its dominant or modal relationship to society is still, with some exceptions by diocese and locality, that of resistance to social change and a dependency on authoritarian controls and traditional powers. Its major officials pursue problem solving mainly through political mechanisms and personal diplomacy. Many differentiated Catholic organizations exist: for students, professional groups, workers, and youth below the university level. But these are not strong centers of autonomous thinking and activity. Many of the ideas and organizational principles that lie at the foundations of these units are quite traditional, at least by the standards of the post-Conciliar era. There are also strong currents of apathy and malaise among organized lay groups as well as among many sectors of the clergy. Membership figures are relatively high by the baptismal measure, but ritual involvement tends to be among the lowest in Latin America, paralleling in broad patterns the tendencies in Uruguay. Laymen who do enter into the work of the Church are tied preponderantly to the roles of "faithful follower" or "clerical auxiliary." Pastoral programs, in the main, are geared to pre-Vatican conceptions of sacramental duty, territorial units, and clerical authority. Most pastors and bishops are oriented to the values of social elites rather than to the workers, the agricultural laborers, or the urban poor.

[14] For historical information on the Argentine Church to the end of the eighteenth century, see de Egaña, *Historia de la Iglesia en la América Española*, pp. 649-751. Materials on the nineteenth and twentieth centuries are provided by Mecham, *Church and State in Latin America*, pp. 225-51; John J. Kennedy, *Catholicism, Nationalism and Democracy in Argentina* (Notre Dame, Ind.: Fides Publishers, Inc., 1958); and Enrique Amato, *La Iglesia en Argentina* (Fribourg, Switzerland: Oficina Internacional de Investigaciones Sociales de FERES, 1965).

Some major attempts to move out of these conservative patterns are being made in the Buenos Aires region, in Cordoba, and the upper estuary cities. These initiatives have gained an increasing publicity, in part due to a series of ecclesiastical incidents wherein new groups—progressives and Colombian-type revolutionaries—have confronted the conservative hierarchy head on.[15] On the whole, however, the Church has not accepted the principles of a pluralistic, modern society nor confronted, in clear terms, the problems attending secularization. It appears that the main leaders of the Church still hold to the ideal of a Catholic society and to notions of power relationships that fit with an older, corporativist model.

Many of the Church's internal tensions and institutional lags are intensified by current political uncertainties in the Argentine nation and by regionally-based styles and identities. When Onganía gained national power in 1966,[16] the top leaders of the Church appeared to be in full support of his government. This semblance of involvement, as political pressure from groups in opposition to the government has increased, placed the Church in an uncomfortable situation.[17] It has thereby eased away from its earlier position, even going so far as to suggest an indirect criticism of the government's policies. Yet sufficient ambiguities remain to render any inference inconclusive. Certain more positive notes have been struck in recent episcopal statements, e.g., in the conclusions of the bishops attending the National Episcopal Conference in late April 1969.[18] These texts stressed the need for the Church to become acquainted with the realities of Argentina's economic and social problems and to undertake responsibility for their solution. These mild stands in support of change did not carry a great deal of public impact. Most of the public's attention regarding the Church was focused on the Rosario "battle" that got underway early in 1969 between Bishop Bolatti and a certain number of innovative priests.

[15] Reports on these recent incidents and the climate of opinion surrounding them are provided in "Dieron un Documento 270 Sacerdotes de Todo el País en Solidaridad con Los 30 Renunciantes de Rosaria," El Clarín (Buenos Aires), April 11, 1969, p. 32; "Renuncias y Cartas: 'No Somos Rebeldes'" (Disconformismo Sacerdotal en Rosario y Tucumán), Análisis, No. 419, March 25-31, 1969, pp. 19-20: and "Rosario: Alto el Fuego?," Primera Plana, No. 324, March 11, 1969, p. 30.

[16] On the early phase of Onganía's leadership, see James W. Rowe, Onganía's Argentina: The First Four Months, Parts I & II, American Universities Field Staff, Inc., New York, N.Y., East Coast South America Series, Vol. XII, Nos. 7 & 8, November, 1966.

[17] Newspapers have reported this shift, e.g., Robert Cox, "Argentina's Church, State Pulling Apart," Washington Post, October 17, 1966.

[18] A discussion and report of this meeting is given in "El Atenuado Eco de Medellín, Conferencia del Episcopado Calma y Alto Nivel," Análisis, No. 424, April 29-May 5, 1969, pp. 8, 10.

Argentine Catholics, despite their weak ritual involvements and spiritual interests, can be motivated to undertake the defense of the Church. This occurs, however, only under special conditions. The Church's influential role in bringing down the Perón government in 1955 is a case in point.[19] The public was already in a mood of disquiet and general anxiety. Uncertainties and fears were part of the whole political picture. When Perón moved against the Church, being incited further by strong reactions on the part of some clergymen, the "people" responded on behalf of the Church. As one participant explained: "I am not a good Catholic, but when they began to burn churches I could not help but take sides."

The Argentine Church is still linked to the State through the Constitution, but it has been freed, recently, from the interferences that came from the long-held *patronato* arrangements. It receives funds from the public treasury and has the freedom to conduct religious instruction in public schools after regular hours. The Church has managed to stave off divorce legislation, and it did manage in the late Fifties to gain full recognition for its university programs. Members of the hierarchy frequently take on public roles, e.g., as mediators between the government and labor groups in strike situations. Churchmen hold many lines of informal access to decision-making groups, and they are frequently called on as consultants by public officials and politicians.

The Argentine Church displays many of the problems of its counterpart in Colombia, though I would judge that the chances for polarization are less in the Argentine situation. A great deal depends on national political developments during the coming years. If certain governmental policies are relaxed, and in particular those that have to do with holding down political "subversion," then some of the current themes of rebellion and protest will undoubtedly diminish. A decline in political tensions would also help to dampen the influence of reactionary sectors within the Church. Innovative steps and calls for religious reform would not be defined as parts of a wider revolutionary movement, but as legitimate aspects of post-Conciliar trends. The political instability of the country tends to heighten anxieties about change; consequently many of the Church's progressive groups and experimental initiatives are quickly thwarted. Even, however, if the political situation grows more liberal and

---

[19] On the evolution of relations between the Church and the Perón government, see Robert J. Alexander, *The Perón Era* (New York: Columbia University Press, 1951), pp. 125 ff.; "Historia del Peronismo: El Apoyo Eclesiástico," *Primera Plana* (Buenos Aires), No. 199, October 18-24, 1966, pp. 36-38; L. Edward Shuck, Jr., "Church and State in Argentina," *The Western Political Quarterly*, II, No. 4, December, 1949.

stable, the Argentine Church will not move quickly into a place of progressive leadership in Latin American Catholicism.

The Mexican Church

In the Mexican Church one finds a special case. Its abrupt and forced disengagement from traditional bases of privilege early in the twentieth century left it without formal ties to the State, without property, and without the right to develop educational institutions. Its possibilities for direct political coalitions or the sponsorship of Church parties were erased by the Constitution of 1917.[20] Deep changes in ritual involvement took place between 1910 and 1930, although latent Catholic sentiment and folk practices maintained strength. In the period following Pius XI's stress on Catholic Action,[21] the Mexican hierarchy began to develop specialized lay groups and units related to growing spheres of secular change in society. These programs were formally intended to be apostolic, i.e., focused on generating new religious commitments and extending Church influence via lay activities, but they turned out to be a series of parallel or insulative-type structures, centered largely around holding loyalties, especially those of the youth, and building certain barriers between Catholics and the wider society.

The Mexican Church thus entered a cautious out-going stage about a generation ago, but it has not moved much beyond that in the interim years. The organized Church is quite traditional, though not politicized. It holds indirect ties, through laymen, with the *Partido de Acción Nacional* (PAN), though there is no way in which to claim that this is a purposeful strategy of the bishops.[22] Occasional and modest attempts are made to relate the Church to some problem of social need, but the major activity takes the form of charity, or traditional welfare services. The Church hierarchy is not well integrated on the national level. Deep regional divisions and cultural identities hold many sectors of the Church in a local framework, thus indicating that national-level structures are relatively weak. Patterns among the laity differ greatly, with the major break between the client-type attachment and the hierarchical auxiliary. Only small groups of laymen are involved in the Church as participat-

[20] See Robert E. Quirk, "Religion and the Mexican Revolution," in *Religion, Revolution, and Reform,* eds. William V. D'Antonio and Frederick B. Pike (New York: Frederick A. Praeger, Inc., 1964), p. 66.

[21] Catholic Action developments in the Mexican Church are analyzed by Ralph C. Beals, *Bureaucratic Change in the Mexican Catholic Church, 1926 to 1950* (Ph.D. dissertation, University of California, Berkeley, 1966).

[22] On PAN's Catholic orientations, see Mecham, *Church and State in Latin America,* p. 412.

ing colleagues. Some experimental developments, especially in the diocese of Cuernavaca, have been initiated: new educational centers for missionary workers, liturgical innovations, and changes in monastic life and the roles of the religious.[23] It must be remembered, of course, that most of these experiments are led by "outsiders"—priests and laymen from Western Europe and the United States. The basic development appears to be in the growth of indigenous vocations to the priesthood and the consequent gains in pastoral (parochial) leadership.[24] The Mexican Church appears to be one that combines a rather traditional and passive hierarchy with two principal types of religious involvement: ritual participation focused on the local Church, and extrasacramental practices that go by the name of folk Catholicism.

Regarding the general trends related to the Church's social role, it is worth noting that the Mexican government and the Party of Revolutionary Institutions (PRI) have removed, if not entirely erased, the kinds of social and ideological stimuli that tend to stimulate a Church in more modern directions. The social needs of the people—education, health, and economic opportunity—are by no means solved, but the state does sponsor institutional development on behalf of these problems. The Church can hardly compete with the government for visibility and influence in areas of social need. No less important, the Church faces few direct threats from religious competition, and far-left value movements are weak. Both factors are important for stimulating a Church toward the modern direction. It appears that the Mexican Church has reached a rather stable plateau in its over-all development. There are no clear indications that it will either regress—moving back to political strategy—or that it will institutionalize the more advanced norms of Vatican II. Although the Mexican Church embraces a strong popular religiosity and is succeeding in building a well-trained indigenous clergy, it is not undergoing far-reaching qualitative changes in either its own structures or in its relations with society.

[23] The Mexican Church's ties to popular cults and devotional activities in local settings suggest that the liturgical sphere may become one of the most important contexts for relating traditional commitments to post-Conciliar themes. One observer makes this point explicitly. See Gaspar Elizondo, "A La Paroisse Universitaire de Mexico: La 'Messe des Jeunes' n'est pas un 'Show,'" *Informations Catholiques Internationales,* No. 336, May 15, 1969, pp. 28-29.

[24] Some of these developments are being reinforced by broader discussions of Church renewal in the major newspapers and journals. Eight authors—intellectuals and journalists—examine problems of change in the Church of Mexico in a symposium entitled "En Torno a La Iglesia de Hoy," *El Día,* Vol. 8, No. 2527, July 1, 1969. The articles are available from the Center of Intercultural Documentation, Cuernavaca, Mexico, as Document 69/149.

Brazil is the largest "Catholic country" in the world and thus its Church can be expected to possess a great deal of visibility in contemporary Latin America. It is a Church that is increasingly identified with a struggle between the "Catholic left" and traditional forces. More than in any of the other four Churches under examination here, or for other Churches in Latin America, the left and the right are quite evenly matched, if not in actual numbers of membership support, at least with regard to influence, persuasiveness, and articulateness. I would judge that the Brazilian Church's polarization has reached proportions that approximate the situation in the French Church between 1880 and 1914, though the issues and tensions are very different. The French split was created by sentiments for and against Republicanism, as well as by loyalties that came into conflict over Gallican and ultramonamtist models of the Church. Today in Brazil, the eye of the storm revolves around the nature of the Church and its mission in society. The left holds that the Church not only has the responsibility but also the right to act forcibly against power structures that appear to be the causes of physical misery, psychological oppression, and social injustices. In order for the Church to claim religious authority or moral leadership, it must enter the concrete struggle for radical structural changes throughout society. The right wing, or "counter-left," holds that the Church should remain aloof from partisan political involvements and give its attention to traditional religious functions. Between these two positions stands a sizeable group of bishops, priests, and laymen who favor rapid change and social relevance for the Church but in terms of strategies that combine emphases of the "social development" and "cultural-pastoral" models. However these progressive forces are being placed under increasing amounts of pressure to take sides in right or left terms, thus helping to sharpen the outlines of the two camps.

Several attempts have been made to trace the historical and political

[25] On the history of the organization of the Brazilian Church, see Alfonso Gregory, *A Igreja No Brasil* (Louvain: FERES, 1965), pp. 99-112. Specific periods and regions are dealt with by Mary Crescentia Thornton, *The Church and Freemasonry in Brazil, 1872-1875. A Study in Regalism* (Washington, D.C.: The Catholic University of America Press, 1948); William J. Coleman, *The First Apostolic Delegation in Rio de Janeiro and Its Influence in Spanish America: A Study in Papal Policy, 1830-1840* (Washington, D.C.: The Catholic University of America Press, 1950); Mecham, *Church and State in Latin America*, pp. 261-79; and M. Ancilla O'Neill, *Tristão de Athayde and the Catholic Social Movement in Brazil* (Washington, D.C.: The Catholic University of America Press, 1939).

roots of the Catholic left in Brazil,[26] so I need not go into detail here. My observations are confined to the broad processes that appear to have brought the Church to its present situation. During Goulart's tenure as President, 1961-1964, the Church's progressive wing began to gain a new confidence and importance. Catholic student groups, a small segment of laymen, and a growing number of priests began to move the Church directly into programs of social reform, especially in support of marginal groups in the countryside of the Northeast. Some of their energies went toward "building up" labor unions; others gave attention to problems of literacy and the formation of the peasant's political conscience; still others concentrated on problems of health and agricultural development. These involvements, especially in the context of Goulart's perceived slide to the left, earned the Catholic reformers a "communist" identity, at least among traditional and conservative leaders in the Church. When the military coup occurred in 1964, the Catholic left, along with other political subversives, came under heavy sanctions, including the imprisonment of some leaders and a withdrawal of government funds for their programs. The Basic Education Movement (MEB) that had developed a broad-based literacy program among the marginal groups almost disappeared.[27] Since literacy training by the Movement had emphasized the development of political and social consciousness, it was viewed as a direct instrument of the political left.

The first few years of the present military regime brought on a relative quiet in the ranks of the Catholic left. From 1967 on, however, things began to change. Dom Helder Camara,[28] Archbishop of Recife and

[26] On the trends and tensions in the contemporary Brazilian Church, see David E. Mutchler, "Roman Catholicism in Brazil," *Studies in Comparative International Development,* Washington University, St. Louis, Missouri, I, No. 8, 1965, 103-17; Thomas G. Sanders, "Catholicism and Development: The Catholic Left in Brazil," in *Churches and States: The Religious Institution and Modernization,* ed. Kalman H. Silvert (New York: American Universities Field Staff, Inc., 1967), pp. 81-99; and Emanuel de Kadt, "Religion, The Church, and Social Change in Brazil," in *The Politics of Conformity in Latin America,* ed. Claudio Veliz (London: Oxford University Press, 1967), pp. 192-220.

[27] The Basic Education Movement is described and analyzed by Thomas C. Bruneau, "Autonomy and Change in the Brazilian Catholic Church," Ms., 1969, Chapter IV, pp. 12-19. Bruneau traces its origins, developments, and identifies the issues that made it nationally controversial. He notes that Cardinal Eugenio Sales of Natal, who originated the program, dropped out of the Movement's directive body in 1963 over the question of its growing "politicization." *Ibid.,* Chapter IV, p. 16.

[28] Certain emphases of Dom Helder Camara's views and proposals are reported in "La Nueva Iglesia de Los Pobres," *Primera Plana* (Buenos Aires, IV, No. 198, October 11-17, 1966, pp. 35-38; and Dom Helder Camara, "La Violence: Option Unique?" *Informations Catholiques Internationales,* No. 312, May 15, 1968, pp. 4-7.

Olinda, and the charismatic leader of the Catholic left, began to re-assert the basic principles of a Church for social justice and used several clashes with the military to drive home the negative features of the status quo. His public criticisms of the regime's policies and of the power establishment more generally, supplemented by proposals for remedying the problems of the poor and the exploited, served as new stimulants to the various groups of the left. Since 1967, members of these groups have become involved in a number of incidents with the government or police that have helped to intensify their solidarity and clarify their identities. These incidents usually receive widespread publicity. This, in turn, stimulates conservative reactions, conflicts among the bishops, and a general heightening of emotions.[29]

This growing polarization, with its accompanying political undertows, may be receiving too much emphasis. Many local situations are not directly affected and some of the leading progressive bishops continue to pursue their own programs of reform. Yet the organization behind the National Conference of Bishops (CNBB) has lost much of its influence and innovative leadership since 1964. Other developments that were carrying forward the themes of Vatican II have grown weak and hesitant. Bruneau's study provides an extraordinarily complete account of these trends and difficulties.[30]

The eventual outcome cannot be presumed at this point since, as in Argentina, a great deal depends on what takes place in the national political system. But barring attempts to predict, the situation in Brazil does hold significant implications for the theses being presented in this book. Before 1961, the year Quadros resigned, the Brazilian Church was developing a very significant sector of progressive influence and showing a new capacity for holding itself autonomous from political structures. Even the more conservative bishops emphasized an "above politics" position. Thus Mutchler reports that strong pressures were placed on the papal nuncio and on the Brazilian bishops in 1959 to declare their support for an anti-communist organization.[31] They refused to do so. Simultaneously the progressive bishops, through such instruments as the Na-

[29] Fourteen of these incidents are described in detail by Thomas C. Bruneau, "Autonomy and Change in the Brazilian Catholic Church," Ms., 1969, Chapter VII.

[30] Ibid. Bruneau's study is based on eighteen months of field research in Brazil, carried out during 1967-1968 and is being prepared as his doctoral dissertation in the Department of Political Science, University of California, Berkeley.

[31] Mutchler, 1965, Studies in Comparative International Development, Vol. I, No. 8, 104.

tional Conference of Bishops, were fostering an image of the Church as an agency of social change. Though funds for new programs came largely from the government, there were no attempts by the latter to interfere with Church policies. Separation of Church and State occurred in 1890.

The chief problem arose, in my judgment, from a tendency among the more progressive leaders of the social reform programs to fuse Church identities with political efforts. Instead of promoting their activities as citizens with Catholic commitments, they appeared to be projecting the Church directly into political struggles. This lack of differentiation, which I believe to be crucial in the Latin American context, prompted reactions among both churchmen and secular elites. This situation intensified the involvements of the grass-roots reformers, giving their activities an even more pronounced political meaning. This broad sequence can be viewed as the diversion of an above-politics movement of Church-based social reform into a politically based movement.

This development is only one of the basic foci of change in the Brazilian Church. Over the past several decades it has also been required to meet stiff competition from non-Catholic religious groups, especially in the major urban areas. Protestant Pentecostals have steadily increased in numbers and influence. Equally important gains have been made by the loosely organized movements of spiritualism. Along other lines, the Church has been steadily undergoing jurisdictional changes, centered around the establishments of new dioceses. Many of the new bishops, unfettered in their work by entrenched administrative practices and traditional lay organizations, are assuming positions of very progressive leadership. In other words the new and open dioceses, often situated in regions that epitomize the economic and social features of traditional society, appear to breed more radical conceptions of the bishop's role. Center-periphery tensions are thereby increased.

The Church in Brazil has broken through traditional styles at many important points. Its size, relative to other national Churches, along with its current role as a center of the Catholic left, give the Brazilian Church a significant leadership role throughout the continent. Modest levels of religious motivation and structural capacities are being freed from established modes, thereby becoming available for new roles in both Church and society. At the moment these newer and more flexible commitments are being partly siphoned into the charismatic adventures of the Christian revolutionaries. This may be temporary. If it is, then there are very definite possibilities that the Brazilian Church will continue its developmental trajectory.

The Chilean Church [32]

The Chilean Church has a reputation for being the most progressive
Church in Latin America.[33] Several important facts add credibility to this
image. Members of the Chilean hierarchy led the way, prior to Vatican
II, in placing the Church and its authority on the side of social change
and human development. It was a Chilean bishop, Manuel Larraín, who
transferred Church lands, in his diocese of Talca, to members of the rural
proletariat. Chilean theologians and social thinkers from the Church
helped to formulate and transmit a Christian conception of "social revolution," giving it concrete expressions through the development of such
programs as *Promoción Popular,* family planning clinics, housing cooperatives, and the like. The Catholic University in Santiago is a major center
for economic research, social studies, and graduate training in the social
sciences. Since 1968, in response to a reform movement of students and
faculty, the administrative structure of the University is being revamped
along lines that provide collegiality in decision making, wider choice in
curricular programs, and flexible departmental structures.

It is also in Chile that concerted attempts have been made to reform
and renew internal Church life. Liturgical reforms got underway prior to
papal authorization in 1962. Several complementary developments deserve mention: an increasing importance is being given to laymen in the
administrative and governmental spheres of the Church; new types of
pastoral work are underway in both middle-class parishes and urban
slums; dioceses linked by regions or metropolitan territories have begun
to develop cooperative pastoral programs; and some headway is being
made in developing anew the role of the deacon (diaconate) in which
laymen serve in pastoral work and in limited sacramental capacities.

The Chilean hierarchy has succeeded in large measure in inserting the
Church and its religious charisma into the culture of modernization and

[32] On the history of the Chilean Church, consult de Egaña, *Historia de la Iglesia
en la América Española,* pp. 199-268; Mecham, *Church and State in Latin America,*
pp. 201-24; Isidoro Alonso *et al., La Iglesia en Chile* (Fribourg, Switzerland: Oficina
Internacional de Investigaciones Sociales de FERES, 1962), pp. 59-61; Luis
Galdames, *A History of Chile,* trans. and ed. Isaac Joslin Cox (New York: Russell
and Russell Inc., 1964) (first published in 1941); and Francisco Vives, "Chile," in
El catolicismo contemporaneo en Hispano-América, ed. Richard Pattee (Buenos
Aires: Editorial Fides, 1951).

[33] For descriptions on the Chilean Church's recent trends, see Ivan Vallier, "Religious Elites: Differentiations and Developments in Roman Catholicism," in *Elites
in Latin America,* eds. Seymour Martin Lipset and Aldo Solari (New York: Oxford
University Press, Inc., 1967), pp. 219-21.

change, and by so doing has helped to give those values greater positive significance. This insertion occurred between 1960 and 1964, a period of intense political competition between the secular left (Popular Front) and the Christian Democrats. Both parties emphasized the imperative of radical structural change in society; both claimed to hold the solution for national development. Through these widespread emphases on "revolutionary change," whether through progressive means or more drastic measures, the whole society and its civic culture became focused on themes of change and development. Christian Democrats, holding public identifications with Catholic ideas and progressive teachings of the Church, helped fuse the principles of change and religion in the secular political arena. In this situation—a lively culture of change, a fusion of Christian-Catholic symbols with national development, and strong competition from the secular left (Communists and Socialists)—the Church leaders were able to hold themselves aloof from partisan politics and at the same time place their symbolic and ideological weight on the side of the "social revolution." Of course, traditional Catholics, including a small number of bishops, viewed this development as scandalous and began to organize themselves in order to counter it. But in the contest the progressive Church held the center of the stage and was able to make, in my judgment, a decisive and positive impact on the national situation. Between 1962 and 1964, the Chilean Church managed to join Catholic values with some of the most advanced notions of national development. At that point the Church reached the first stages of what I have referred to earlier as the new "cultural" connection.

This emerging cultural role on the part of the hierarchy was paralleled by important structural developments within the Church. Here I refer to the establishment of diocesan and parish councils, the inclusion of laymen in synodical gatherings, new emphases on religious training in the local church, e.g., bible study circles, modified *cursillos*, and liturgical instruction, as well as a gradual promotion of the idea that Chile was no longer a Christian society, thus requiring of the priest and layman new types of secular roles. Progressive bishops have begun to draw laymen into decision-making and planning activities, freeing themselves for a more pastoral role. This trend has received symbolic meaning in instances where bishops have moved out of their comfortable episcopal residences into poorer districts, thus enhancing possibilities for building close relations with marginal peoples.

Subsequent events have raised new problems for this emerging "new Church." For one thing the Christian Democrats have lost measures of popular support. Second, the Party has developed an important internal division between those who want to move further left, including open collaboration with the Popular Front, and those identified with President Frei who emphasize a more reformist and gradualist strategy of national change. In addition the Church lost, by the accidental death of bishop Manuel Larraín, one of its most convincing progressive leaders. In the midst of these shifts and losses, new groups of Christian revolutionaries have emerged, such as the Young Church Movement (*Movimiento Iglesia Joven*), which identify with their counterparts in Brazil, Colombia, Peru, and Mexico. In the face of these protests and revolutionary incidents, many of which involve direct assaults on the hierarchy, progressive leaders are beginning to take firm stands and thus are becoming identified with the establishment.

The year 1970 brings the important national elections in which the Christian Democrats may be defeated. Should the Church attempt to use its influence to buttress the more conservative sector of the Christian Democratic Party, or move in other ways to legitimize partisan political forces, it could seriously interrupt its recently won position on the cultural-pastoral trajectory. In short, it appears that there are new opportunities for the Church to become entangled in the public political arena. Its adaptations during the next few years will be decisive both for its own long-range development and perhaps for Latin American Catholicism.

SYSTEMATIC COMPARISONS

The profiles of the five Church systems call attention to broad patterns of controversy, normative change, and specialized programs. Similarities of these kinds tend, however, to hide the basic issue, namely, the degree to which new structures and roles are being institutionalized. In this section I reduce the scope of my observations to certain aspects of change in the Church which, for my purposes, ground the essential differences among the five national systems. I have selected four clusters of change as comparative categories: [34] (1) the consolidation of the episcopal role as one of socioethical leadership, (2) the extent of developments in interdiocesan and national-level infrastructures, (3) the strength of pastoral and congregational patterns in local church life, and (4) the degree to which an integrated Catholic-secular role is being institutionalized for laymen. These four dimensions hold an integral relation to the features of the cultural-pastoral model identified in Chapter Four. My objective is to rank the five Churches, in qualitative terms, on these four dimensions.

[34] These dimensions amplify and extend my work in an earlier article: Ivan Vallier, "Church 'Development' in Latin America: A Five-Country Comparison," *Journal of Developing Areas*, I, No. 4, July, 1967, 461-76.

Dimension 1. *The consolidation of the episcopal role as one of socioethical leadership.* Although all of the national episcopal bodies in the five countries have formulated public statements that reflect post-Conciliar ideas or that define the Church as having responsibility for facilitating change in society, some of these pronouncements are more ritualistic than others. In addition, major differences exist with respect to the congruence between public statements and everyday behaviors. Judging from what I perceive about these behavioral patterns as well as the kinds of credibility that rank-and-file members attach to episcopal statements, I find a distinct bimodal pattern that places Chile and Brazil on the more consolidated side and the Churches of Mexico, Argentina, and Colombia on the token or minimal side.

Dimension 2. *The extent of growth in interdiocesan and national-level infrastructures.* This awkward phrase refers to organizational and integrative structures that are emerging alongside and above the segmental pattern created by bounded dioceses and missionary territories. Although dioceses continue to be the major decision-making structures, many new problems that flow from regional, national, and functional centers are not addressed by local bishops. Under these conditions, new coordinative and problem-solving elites are emerging, giving their energies to planning, research, special types of education, and social problems. The growth of interdiocesan and national nuclei have a twofold importance for Church development: first, they add to the Church's capacities to move flexibly on issues and problems of national scope; second, they add bases of support and organizational leadership to the initiatives that progressive bishops take at the cultural level. Chile and Brazil appear to lead the way in these new developments, with only weak showings in Argentina, Mexico, and Colombia.

Dimension 3. *The strength of pastoral and congregational patterns in local church life.* This refers to the development of the priest's role as pastoral leader and colleague, as well as to the ways in which the symbolic and group bases of religious life are changing. None of the Churches shows strong indications of institutionalization in these respects. Incipient shifts are being made in Mexico and Chile. There are only minimal indications in Brazil and Argentina. Colombia, relative to the other four, evidences no changes along these lines. While it is valid to claim that there are signs of "new life" in pastoral and parochial activities in all of the countries, I do not consider scattered instances of experimental liturgies and clandestine "house masses" indicators of solid structural change. Instead I refer to efforts which involve the re-training of the clergy, the growth of authentic decision-making roles for laymen, and the rearrangement of parish boundaries as means of bringing religious activities into closer correspondence with the sociological bases of the local area. One should also recognize that there is a difference between the official, Church-wide program of liturgical reform and the development of pastoral-congregational structures. The official revision of the liturgy to include the vernacular and the appointments of lay readers for delivering the scriptural lesson do not, in my judgment, constitute major structural changes.

Dimension 4. *The degree to which an integrated Catholic-secular role is being institutionalized for laymen.* My estimates on this complex variable are based on three types of indicators: (1) the growth of orientations and behaviors among laymen that imply a rejection of confessional organizations (Catholic Action movements, Christian labor unions, Catholic schools, etc.) in favor of secular associations and pluralistic involvements; (2) the emergence of an ethical definition of religion action in the world in place of traditional emphases on rule observance; and (3) an approach to life that views man as having a responsibility to reshape human society rather than seeing it as part of an unchangeable natural order. These developments, along with related tendencies and expectations, appear to be altering the role of the Catholic in society. On one level it involves a re-alignment between a person's religious status ("Catholic") and his other major statuses, occupational, political, etc. Whereas the traditional configuration has tended to place the religious status in the position of an overarching referent, stimulating a person to approach secular roles in terms of Catholic conceptions and codes, the emerging pattern places the religious status alongside secular ones in a specialized and differentiated way. On this basis secular roles, and thus secular spheres more generally, gain a normative autonomy in relation to processes of modernization.

At another level, the layman's traditional obligations to uphold confessional and proscriptive rules in the course of his secular activities are being replaced by an internalized set of values and action principles that serve as general guides for relating religious and secular priorities. Large measures of autonomy and freedom are given to the person for making behavioral decisions. Both processes—the realignment of statuses and the reliance on internalized controls—help extricate the person from confessional anchorages and also provide a basis for integrating secular and Christian values.

There is no adequate, empirical basis on which I can make detailed judgments about variations in the five countries. As to estimates, I think Mexico and Chile are showing some changes toward a new role for the Catholic in society. Argentina, especially in the Buenos Aires region, is also moving this way. Brazil and Colombia are weakest. My reasoning involves several referents. In Mexico, Catholics have learned to live in an environment that is potentially hostile to the Church. Secular roles and public involvements are assumed without extending confessional considerations into expectations and encounters. I would judge these postures to be most developed among people involved in professional, technical, and political occupations. Chile appears to be taking a similar course, but for different reasons. There I think the influence of progressive Church leadership, plus the growth of an educated middle class, hold most significance. Argentina's middle class is undoubtedly larger than in Chile, but members of the professional and technical strata have not had the encouragement from Church leaders that would help them break through confessional identities. The case of Brazil, which I place on the very low end of the scale, is less clear. Although a considerable middle class is emerging in the metropolitan areas and progressive episcopal leadership is influential, I think that Brazilians hold a more confessional outlook than their counterparts in the three countries mentioned above. There is less willingness to give up a conception of the Church as a diffuse, public agency of orientation and control. This may have something to do with the polarizations that are currently taking place. In Colombia the integration of the secular with a specialized type of Catholic role is weakest. Catholicism intrudes into every major role system, and the majority of laymen hold to expectations that reinforce the Church's confidence in public life. I offer these as tentative estimates.

A Preliminary Index

The foregoing assessments and comparisons can now be drawn together in a rudimentary table summarizing my evaluations of the national Churches on each of the four dimensions. I assign numerical quantities to each of five ordinal categories as follows: an absence of noticeable institutionalization is scored as zero; minimal institutionalization is scored as one; incipient institutionalization is scored as two; partial institutionalization is scored as three; considerable institutionalization is scored as four. An over-all index of Church development, based on features of the cultural-pastoral model, is obtained for each Church by adding the number assigned on the four dimensions.

There is no intention in this comparative analysis to associate value judgments with variations in "development." The purpose of this measurement strategy is to indicate that five of the key Church systems in Latin America vary quite dramatically in their internal features and in their relations to the broader processes of social change. By locating the Church that is most "developed" in terms of the criteria used, the conditions of national Church change can be studied as a sequence of religious de-

Table 7.1

Variations in Church Development Scores

National Church Systems

Comparative Dimensions	Argen-tina	Brazil	Chile	Colom-bia	Mexico
1. New episcopal role	1	3	3	1	1
2. New infrastructures	1	3	3	1	1
3. Pastoral-congrega-tional mode	1	1	2	0	2
4. Integrated Catholic-secular role	2	1	3	1	3
National developmental scores	5	8	11	3	7

Code: 0–absence of institutionalization
1–minimal institutionalization
2–incipient institutionalization
3–partial institutionalization
4–consolidated: considerable institutionalization

velopment. It is quite clear that the Chilean Church stands in a distinct position of high development within this framework; given the common context, the sociological task now is to uncover the conditions that have led to this "deviant" level of development.

THE CHURCH IN CHILE: AN EXPLANATION

In terms of qualitative comparative observations, the Church in Chile stands highest on the developmental index. The question to be answered is, Why is the Chilean more "developed" than the other national Churches? Two types of analysis can be used to answer this question: first, an examination of the correlates of Church development in Chile's national life that differ from conditions in the other countries discussed. Are there social, economic, or cultural variables of a distinct non-Church nature that are more prevalent in Chile than in the other four countries? If so, do they have a meaningful relation to Church development? The second line of analysis involves an examination of the internal dynamics of the Chilean Church to find out if certain special events or processes have occurred in the recent history of the Church. At the present stage, it would be impossible to locate a single cause of the Chilean Church's "high" development; but it is certainly possible to identify certain "facilitating," perhaps even "sufficient" conditions.

Distinctive Features of Chile as a Nation and Society

Physically, Chile is the smallest of the five countries examined; moreover, it has the smallest population in absolute numbers—a population heavily concentrated in the Santiago–Valparaiso–Concepción triangle.[35] Chile's population is not characterized historically by major foreign immigration waves or contemporaneously by deep ethnicoracial cleavages, as are the other four countries in various ways.

In socioeconomic terms, Chile stands high on indexes of industrialization and urbanization, as do Mexico, Argentina, and key sections of Brazil, especially the south.[36] Many observers consider Chile to be a special case in relation to "economic growth potential," although its chronic inflation and incapacity to raise agricultural productivity to a level that would reduce food imports do not warrant assigning it to a high ranking on an economic development scale. Chile's social profile evinces a large and growing middle class; however, this hardly distinguishes it, particularly when compared to Argentina, Mexico, and major sections of Brazil.

Chile's Catholic membership as indexed by baptism is in the same range as Argentina, Mexico, and Brazil (85–90 percent) but lower than Colombia's (95–98 percent). According to standard measures of ritual participation, Chilean Catholics behave in much the same way as do Catholics in Argentina, Mexico, and Brazil.[37] The ratio of clergy to population is somewhat higher in Chile than in any other country, approximately one priest for every 3000 members.[38] The Chilean Church has gained a more national ecclesiastical base in terms of organized dioceses than have Colombia and Brazil where large areas still exist as missionary territories.

Except for the physical size of the country, the more concentrated distribution and relative ethnic homogeneity of the people, Chile does not seem unique in Latin America along the major social dimensions discussed. Four additional variables, however, bear special mention: (1) governmental stability (or "political development"), (2) Communist

[35] Based on recent electoral patterns and census figures, as noted in Orville G. Cope, "The 1964 Presidential Election in Chile: The Politics of Change and Access," *Inter-American Economic Affairs*, XIX, Spring, 1966, p. 6 ff.

[36] Consult *Urbanization in Latin America*, ed. Philip M. Hauser (New York: International Documents Service, Columbia University Press, 1961), pp. 94, 114.

[37] Houtart and Pin, *The Church and the Latin American Revolution*, pp. 164-75.

[38] Figures on the ratio of clergy to population for all the Latin American countries are given in Gustavo Pérez and Isaac Wust, *La Iglesia en Colombia* (Fribourg, Switzerland: Oficina Internacional de Investigaciones Sociales de FERES, 1961), Cuadro 42, p. 141; for example: Argentina 1:4530, Chile 1:2980 (the highest ratio), Colombia 1:3810, Brazil 1:6380, Mexico 1:5380.

strength, (3) Pentecostal strength, and (4) Christian Democratic strength. A brief discussion of each of these will demonstrate some sources of uniqueness in the national society.

Chile's national political system, indexed by its relative stability, the capacities of the electoral system to mobilize and transfer power, and by such things as the restraint of the military, is frequently cited by competent observers of Latin America as a model of progressive political development.[39]

Two other characteristics must be added to this exceptional political pattern. First of all, Chile is one of Latin America's major centers for the organized secular left (Communists and Socialists). The Chilean "left" has more public visibility, electoral support, and ideological prominence than do leftist factions in any of the other four countries. Alexander notes that the Chilean Communists "have been a factor of importance in their country's politics longer and more consistently than have their comrades in any other country of Latin America." [40] The second distinctive feature of the Chilean political scene is the strength of the Christian Democratic party (PDC). Beginning in the mid-1930s as a small nucleus of Catholic university students who broke with the Conservative party, it began to take on national importance after 1938 when the Popular Front alliance gained national power.[41] The Chilean PDC originally drew its central ideological principles and organizational strategies from its European counterparts, but it has now developed its own political style. Like several other Christian Democratic parties in Latin America, the PDC is closer to "the Center-Left in Italy or with leaders of the as yet submerged radical Christian movements in Spain or Portugal" than to "the Erhards or the Scelbas. . . ." [42]

The fourth aspect of Chile's national life that deserves special mention is the rapid increase in the Protestant Pentecostal sects. Brazil is the only one of the other countries in which the Pentecostals have made exceptional gains. However, Protestants in Brazil are only 4.3 percent of the

---

[39] A recent comparative study of political development in 66 countries, including those of Latin America, gives Chile the highest rating for the continent. See Phillips Cutright, "National Political Development: Measurement and Analysis," *American Sociological Review*, XXVIII, April, 1963, 253-64, especially Fig. 1, p. 258.

[40] Robert J. Alexander, *Communism in Latin America* (New Brunswick, N.J.: Rutgers University Press, 1957), p. 177.

[41] For the development of Chile's Christian Democratic party, see Ernest Halperin, *Nationalism and Communism in Chile* (Cambridge, Mass.: M.I.T. Press, 1964), esp. Chapter 5, "The Christian Democratic Alternative," pp. 178-205; also Alberto Edwards Vivas and Eduardo Frei Montalva, *Historia de los partidos políticos chilenos* (Santiago, Chile: Editorial del Pacífico, S.A., 1949).

[42] Hugh O'Shaughnessy, "The Chilean Experiment," *Encounter*, XXV, September, 1965, 89.

population; within this Protestant population, the Pentecostals make up an estimated 58 percent. In Chile, however, Protestants comprise approximately 10 percent of the population and roughly 85 percent of these are Pentecostals.[43] Thus, in this respect, as in national political development, strength of the secular left, and strength of the Christian Democrats, Chile is quite distinctive comparatively.

What bearing do these four patterns have on the Chilean Church's greater development as an agency of social change? Four observations may be made: (1) Chile's strength at the level of national political institutions reduces the tendencies of the Catholic Church to enter directly into the political arena, thus freeing it to build its image as a universal institution or above politics. This inference, although tentative, derives from a more general Latin American pattern in which political instability and Church involvement in politics are correlated. (2) The strength of the Christian Democratic party, which is Catholic but not confessional, tends to function as a second restraint on the Church as a political agent, since many ideas and loyalties to the Catholic Church can be expressed in this party. (3) The strength of the secular left, and the extraordinary symbolic importance of Communism in particular, pose a deep threat to the Church's social status and its system of religio-ideological controls. Moreover, the fact that the Chilean political system is not easily vulnerable to extraconstitutional pressures prevents the Church from working for anti-Communist statutes; quite the contrary, the "new Church" elites realize that the "secular left" must be met in the spheres of social and "religious" activity. (4) Pentecostal strength constitutes another unavoidable threat to the Church, for these sects not only make gains in the lower classes where the Church is weak but also offer Christian-based values and goals, which help to integrate these classes into urban–industrial society, via the occupational, secular performance complex.

These observations lead to two conclusions about the Chilean situation and Church development. First, the nation's political stability and the growth of the Christian Democratic party serve in combination to provide a "buffer" between the official Church and the political arena; second, the Church is heavily threatened by the growth of aggressive competing "religio-moral" value movements (Communists and the Pentecostals). This threat stimulates the new elites to give the Church's manifest ideology concrete bases in action programs. These two complexes—the presence of a "buffer" that reduces the Church's possible political involve-

[43] Emilio Willems, "Protestantism and Culture Change in Brazil and Chile," in *Religion, Revolution, and Reform,* eds. D'Antonio and Pike, 93-108; statistics from pp. 95, 97, 101; Christian Lalive d'Epinay, *El Refugio de las Masas: Estudio sociológico del protestantismo chileno* (Santiago: Editorial del Pacífico, S.A., 1968).

ments and, second, the presence of a deep threat from competing secular and religious value movements—constitute the basic *external* conditions for Church development.

We can now turn to some of the important *internal* conditions which, in conjunction with the *external* conditions noted above, appear to be helpful in formulating an explanation for the deviant case. Here account needs to be taken of at least three sets of events, all occurring within the Chilean Church over the past 35 years. (1) Between 1929 and 1940, a priest-led reform movement emerged within the Church to challenge the conservative hierarchy on religious grounds and to stimulate a lay-type, Catholic-based, political movement of the left, the forerunner of the present Christian Democratic party. The momentum of this movement derived largely from the efforts of one man, Alberto Hurtado, S.J.[44] Hurtado's impeccable religious life, his continued assertion that Christian commitment demanded a commitment to social reform, his insight into the functions of a Catholic-inspired, but nonconfessional, lay-led political reform movement, and his charisma, which attracted talented young men to the priesthood, gave an exceptionally strong push to the Church's whole developmental sequence.

(2) Several episcopal appointments[45] between 1939 and 1960 developed support within the hierarchy for such efforts as Hurtado's to separate the Church from its traditional anchorages (upper status, conservatism, corporativism), and transform it into an ally of change and the common people. José María Caro Rodríguez, appointed Archbishop of Santiago in 1939, was not a compulsive progressive; but he nevertheless encouraged the new movements in the Church and came to their defense when conservative bishops tried silencing or eliminating tactics. Also in 1939, Manuel Larraín Errazuriz assumed the episcopal chair for the diocese of Talca. Touched by the same reforming urge as his friend Padre Hurtado, Larraín quickly emerged as a central figure in the growing "new" sector of the Church. At his untimely death in 1966, Larraín had gained an international reputation for his progressive ideas, his practical genius for Church "politics" and administration, and for his undeniably central role in pulling the Church into its new role. Although he is most commonly associated with his land reform program[46] through

---

[44] Alejandro Magnet, *El Padre Hurtado,* 3rd ed. (Santiago, Chile: Editorial del Pacífico, S.A., 1957). Additional biographical information was gained by interviewing former colleagues and students of Hurtado's.

[45] The evolution of episcopal leadership in Chile is recorded in Poblete, *et al., La Iglesia en Chile,* pp. 153-68.

[46] For an evaluation of these Church programs of land redistribution, see William C. Thiesenhusen, *Chile's Experiments in Agrarian Reform* (Madison, Wis.: University of Wisconsin Press, 1966), Chapters 2-5.

which Church properties have been made available to *campesinos*, Larraín actually symbolized the front-line changes in the whole Church: ideological, theological, and ecclesiastical. Cardinal Caro died in 1959, leaving the central episcopal see vacant. After a brief interim, Raul Silva Henríquez, recently named to the see of Valparaiso, was moved to Santiago as the new cardinal. Pope John XXIII's influence was already apparent, for Silva Henríquez turned out to be a champion for the "new Church." Under his leadership, the Chilean Church entered an unprecedented phase of national mobilization. Through these special episcopal orientations toward social change, the Chilean Church has realized a second important internal condition: the emergence of strategically placed progressive bishops (archbishops, cardinals).

(3) Between 1955 and 1964, the Church in Chile was able to draw from within its own ranks and from Churches in north Europe a select elite of clerical and lay experts. On the one hand, these experts were well suited to give the "new" sector's aspirations an ideological-theological grounding; on the other, they were capable of undertaking the practical and scientific tasks involved in establishing key programs and projects connecting ideology to social problems. This addition of skills and capacities make up a third distinctive internal condition: the recruitment and development of a stratum of professional cosmopolitan Church experts.

Having cited the more important *external* features of the Chilean situation that are judged to be centrally related to Chilean Church development, and the key *internal* changes that have equal importance for this change, an over-all hypothesis on Latin American Church development can now be formulated. On one level, we give special importance to national political conditions that help to keep the Church separate from direct political involvements. On another level, particular significance must be attached to the presence of aggressive value movements that deeply threaten the Church's religious-moral status. Internally, emphasis is given to the sequential emergence of (1) priest-sponsored religious reforms that promote the norm of social justice and institutional change; (2) strategic episcopal appointments providing hierarchical backing for the transformation of the Church into an agency of social reform; and (3) the recruitment of theological, sociological, and administrative experts who are capable, once the theological and hierarchical ground has been laid, of linking the general aspirations of the "new Church" to effective programs in the national society. No one set of factors is the key. Nor would I hold that these are the "necessary" conditions. Together, however, they do make up one important complex of "sufficient" conditions.

SUMMARY

Latin American Catholicism possesses distinctive sociological features relative to the Catholicisms of Northwestern Europe, the British Isles, and the United States. But these geo-cultural differences represent only one level of study and analysis. More important for present purposes are the patterned variations that are developing *within* the Latin American Church. Five national Church systems have been described briefly with reference to a theoretical model of evolutionary change and Church development. More focused comparisons were made on four broad dimensions, followed by a preliminary scoring operation that assigned numbers to each of the five Churches. Although this measuring technique allowed for a maximum developmental score of 16, none of the Churches merits that reading. The highest score was given to the Church in Chile: a score of 11. I then turned to the problem of explaining the Chilean pattern with attention to both contextual and internal factors. These efforts provide one basis on which the study of institutional change may be pursued further.

A threefold objective has guided this book: (1) to identify the basic features of traditional Catholicism, with particular attention to the kinds of control systems that operate and how these affect corporate problem solving; (2) to identify the underlying principles of newer strategies of influence and to relate them to the traditional Church as part of a general model of evolutionary change; and (3) to report cross-national variations in the extent of institutionalization of new structures, with further attention to the conditions related to the differences. In the course of pursuing these objectives, several substantive problems have been examined: the bearing of the Church's traditional adaptive strategies on political instability, the ways in which more recent models of influence and control affect the Church's linkages with society, the role of emerging patterns of episcopal leadership and interdiocesan centers of organization for extricating the Church from the political arena, and the ways in which the trend toward a pastoral-congregational emphasis in the local church augments flexible associational ties and the integration of religious and secular roles.

These topics gain their significance from a theoretical position that views Catholicism's relationship to society in terms of evolving systems of control and influence, each of which ties the Church to particular groups and structures in the

CHAPTER EIGHT

Conclusions

wider society. Accordingly the problem of delimiting change in the Church and that of assessing its significance for sociopolitical development, or "modernization," consists in identifying its basic mechanisms of social control, or the institutional and interpersonal arrangements that are developed (or defended) to make its influence felt on individuals, groups, or secular spheres. Instead of approaching the relationship of Catholicism to modernization in terms of the orientations and attitudinal sets of the "typical Catholic," I have focused on the structural features of the Church, its relationships to cultural and historical situations, and the kinds of consequences—direct and indirect—its corporate efforts to achieve and hold influence have for the total society. This perspective assumes that the Church's sacred mission stimulates its officials and elites to pursue calculated and continuous programs of social control.

The Church's mission is totalistic in that all men are either actual or potential targets of religious concern. But this formal mandate, believed to be assigned by Christ, is carried forward on the basis of diverse theories and various kinds of structural formats: proselytizing campaigns, educational systems, sacramental schedules, mass media networks, welfare services, research and planning agencies, associations for youth, adults, and class-based groups, etc. These diversified enterprises tend to evolve through time as integrated systems of religious influence. Correspondingly the extensiveness and scope of these endeavors, as in Latin America, imply that the Church's control systems are not peripheral and occasional components of social life, but pervasive and pivotal phenomena. In short, whether the Church is anchored in control systems that involve the State, political elites, and extensive landholdings or in those that emphasize ethical leadership, differentiated religious congregations, and the sacredness of temporal engagements on the part of the laity does make a difference for societal change.

THE SIGNIFICANCE OF STRUCTURAL DIFFERENTIATION

Structural differentiation between the Church and major secular spheres is a basic condition of Church development. Church development, in turn, is one, but not the sole, condition for the continuing modernization of society. What are some of the factors that stimulate differentiation? And how do the outcomes alter the Church's position in society?

Differentiation is a product of corporate sequences of problem solving.[1]

[1] For more extended discussions and applications of the process of structural differentiation, consult Talcott Parsons and Neil J. Smelser, *Economy and Society* (Glencoe, Illinois: The Free Press, 1956), esp. Chapter V; Neil J. Smelser, *Social Change in the Industrial Revolution: An Application of Theory to the British Cotton Industry,*

Problem solving, in turn, is forced upon a given system when its conventional ways of meeting competition prove ineffective. Competition is particularly problematic when the opposition begins to demonstrate that its procedures are more effective than the Church itself in achieving religious values. Interestingly, the Church has not been forced, until quite recently, to compete for religious ascendancy. Its competitive problem has consisted mainly in defending itself against political groups who claimed that its scope of involvement in society was too wide. This challenged the social, economic, and political features of the Church, not its core religious features. This distinction between political competition and religious competition is extremely important, since it is the latter that is forcing the Church to turn toward a specialized religious role—a process I consider to be of fundamental significance for the whole problem of modernization.

From this perspective, the growth of other "religions" in Latin America during the past 50 years emerges as a central stimulant to development in the Church. The rise of the Pentecostal sects and the growth of Communism brought a new dimension to the problem-solving tasks of Roman Catholicism. Both these movements espoused values and goals that can be identified with core Christian teachings: equality, brotherhood, justice, and "freedom" from various types of bondage. Radical conceptions of salvation accompanied these value emphases—the Pentecostals focusing on other-worldly salvation through worldly perfection, the Communists concerned with salvation in this world through a revolutionary change of institutions. Both movements, in turn, accepted the principle of alienation from the existing society; hence, both movements stimulated social tensions and a response of apprehensiveness from those who represented the status quo. Finally, both movements began to develop organizational formats that provided marginal people with opportunities for social solidarity, leadership training, and emotional expression.

I do not intend to claim that the Pentecostals and the Communists are entirely comparable as collective movements; that would be both naïve and theoretically unfruitful. What I do want to underline is that both movements began to challenge Roman Catholicism at the "religious" level, i.e., in terms of its conceptions of salvation, its claims to represent

---

1770-1840 (Chicago: University of Chicago Press, 1959); Ivan Vallier, "Structural Differentiation, Production Imperatives and Communal Norms: The Kibbutz in Crisis," Social Forces, 40, 3, March, 1962, pp. 233-42; Shmuel N. Eisenstadt, The Political Systems of Empires: The Rise and Fall of the Bureaucratic Societies (New York: The Free Press of Glencoe, Crowell-Collier, 1963); Talcott Parsons, Societies: Evolutionary and Comparative Perspectives (Englewood Cliffs, N. J.: Prentice-Hall, Inc., 1966); and Robert M. Marsh, Comparative Sociology: A Codification of Cross-Societal Analysis (New York: Harcourt, Brace and World, 1967).

religious truth, and its capabilities to reach the common man. These pressures could not be met by trying to maintain constitutional clauses that guarantee Catholicism a position as the official religion, nor by elaborating Catholic schools, Catholic trade unions, and Catholic parties. Instead, they required efforts that focused on the creation and articulation of general values, the providing of opportunities for primary forms of social solidarity, and the opening of ways for integrating the rank and file into a wider system of collective meaning and social rewards.

The Church begins to specialize in religious activities, and thus remove itself from wider involvements and concerns, when it confronts religious types of competition. In Chile, as discussed earlier, these types of religious competition have been especially strong. Both the Pentecostals and the Communists hold significant positions of influence in that society. The Catholic answer to communism is found in the development of the Christian Democratic party—a development that originated among Catholic laymen and that has managed to maintain autonomy from the institutional Church. The Catholic answer to Pentecostalism is only emerging, being demonstrated in part by the incipient congregational trend and in part by the growth of flexible types of lay leadership roles, expressive retreat programs, and revivalistic campaigns. Both these problem-solving endeavors have helped to facilitate important processes of differentiation and integration. The rise of the Christian Democratic party helped to break the traditional fusion between the clerical stratum and politics, thus fostering a type of reform-oriented lay politics that served the progressive sector of the Church without pushing it into direct politics. The growth of the Pentecostals has pushed religious leaders to examine the Church as a Christian-religious system and to promote pastoral and spiritual forms of leadership.[2] Both movements, in turn, have stimulated the Church to undertake long-range planning and to articulate goals that pertain to the society as a whole. In short, the organization of the Chilean Church is being extended upward from the diocese to a national center, on the one hand, and downward from the diocese and parish into the grass roots, on the other. This two-way extension in its role system is paralleled by a general process of differentiation between Church structures and secular spheres.

These observations suggest that communism, Pentecostalism, or their functional equivalents are of extraordinary importance for the long-range

[2] As the Church undergoes differentiation from structural centers in the secular sphere it moves toward a new set of integrative ties to the total culture through its religious capacities. I have dealt with this process of extraction and re-entry in Ivan Vallier, "Extraction, Insulation, and Re-Entry: Toward a Theory of Religious Change," in Henry A. Landsberger, ed., *The Church in Latin America* (Notre Dame, Indiana: University of Notre Dame Press, forthcoming).

process of change and modernization in Latin America. That importance does not lie so much in their direct contribution, i.e., the role of communism in fostering social revolution or the role of the Pentecostals in producing Calvinist ascetics, but rather in the ways these value movements push the Church toward religious specialization, thus extricating it from secular involvements and traditional adaptive emphases. At the same time, the Pentecostals are more important than the communists, and for two reasons. First, the Pentecostals emerge directly out of the Christian tradition and consequently challenge Catholicism at its most vulnerable center. Second, the Pentecostals are apolitical; their collective activities are limited to strictly religious issues, and thus carry no direct political meanings or implications. On the other hand, the Communists may challenge the Catholic elites at the value level; but, being a full-fledged political movement, they tend to stimulate countervailing political responses. Where the Church lacks the insulating mechanisms of a strong, reformist Christian Democratic party, the Communist threat pushes it toward the pole of reaction. When this occurs, the Church remains firmly imbedded in the political sphere, which is the distinguishing criterion of traditional Catholicism.

Conditions Other than Religious Competition

Religious competition appears to be one of the main stimulants in producing a Church that is either neutral to or facilitative of social change in society; however, several other important factors deserve brief mention. Of first importance is the existence of a relatively large industrial sector with strong, politically organized groups championing or favoring national policies of change. The Church, as a rule, is relatively weak among these industrially related groups. Its anxiety over these problems has been emphasized in such themes as "de-Christianization" and "the loss of the urban proletariat." At the same time, the presence of strong organized forces attending to economic and political issues stimulates ideological and action efforts in the Church. It is drawn into contact with the central issues of the urban-industrial society and responds by direct attempts to meet the threats implied. The focus changes from territorial and defensive styles to "offense," or selective action along functional lines.

The second social condition that fosters a more open and flexible Church is the rising importance of marginal status groups that have heretofore remained outside both the political system and the central life of the Church. In South America, these are mainly the *campesinos* and the urban poor. By going after these groups, the Church is placed once again under the burden of combining new forms of action with normative appeals that bear directly on the sociopolitical needs of the people involved. In doing so, it cuts many of its ties with the traditional elites and, as well, scuttles a certain range of its traditional structures and problem-solving models. The Church initiates a new level of organized action focused on meeting demands that are directly tied to the process of societal change.

However, it is the third social factor that holds the most significance for transferring or levering the Church from a traditional (short-term, *ad hoc*, and conservative) style to a more modern role; namely, the need to back its new efforts by an ideology that combines both principles or symbols of change and universal human values. It can no longer pretend to reach the poor or the worker or the peasant by appeals to supernatural salvation alone. These functions are taken over by the Protestant sects, spiritualist movements, etc. Instead, it is placed under burden to underwrite, and if possible, give meaning to central secular values. In doing so, it undergoes a dual process: (1) On the cultural and normative level, it shifts its emphasis from particularistic and confessional interests to the human needs of all men; (2) on the organizational level, its procedures and structures shift from informal maneuverings and defensive patterns toward a corporate rationality that emphasizes long-range goals, flexible programs and services, and the resocialization of laymen to roles that combine secular and religious norms. This shift from a concern with the level of participation in religious rituals to the Christian's involvement in society helps to free the Church from confessional anxieties. It finds that the Catholic or Christian can be both in modern society and in the Church. The basic orientation in the past assumed that to be "in modern society" meant to be out of the Church, or vice versa. This distinction between sacred and secular becomes insignificant in the new Church.

From the side of society, and nonreligious institutions, this evolutionary pattern progressively frees secular activities from the dominance of Catholic norms, segregates political affairs from ecclesiastical legacies, and opens the way for new social identities and solidarity bases to emerge. In turn, the society may receive inputs from the religious sector, in the form of value statements and religiously linked motivations, that positively assist progressive secular elites in their efforts to institutionalize change and to achieve national or regional developmental goals. Put another way, the secular sphere is gradually freed from the obstructive tendencies of the Church but also stands the chance of gaining some degrees of positive support for secular goals. The Church, in turn, reaches a point where its more specialized religious and symbolic emphases bring it valuable types of recognition, prestige, and influence. The important point is that these rewards from society do not depend on direct involvements in the political, economic, and educational sectors of society. In fact, the more the

Church stays in its own bailiwick, the greater the probabilities that its rewards will increase and social development will occur.

These observations can be put into proposition form: (1) the greater the scope and imbeddedness of an organized religion's control apparatus in a society, the greater its consequences for the course of events and changes in society; (2) the greater the traditionalizing content of the actions that make up the religion's control system, the greater the religion's obstructive potential in a situation of change; (3) the stronger the threats and competitiveness of a religious nature in society, the higher the probabilities that a religion will shift its control strategies to specialized religious emphases—symbolic leadership, differentiated religious associations, and depth forms of religious socialization; (4) the more a religion assumes these specialized religious roles in a society, the greater the possibilities for innovation and change in the secular spheres.

The specialization of the religious system in terms of its organized activities and symbolic emphases does not mean that it loses relevance in society or forfeits its chances for influence and prestige. On the contrary: It enhances its charismatic potential, because it is then possible for it to function as a source of spiritual and moral leadership, and it realizes key roles in society through its association with problems of cultural development and the problems of meaning of the people. Too often, it is assumed that the processes of specialization and differentiation in society reduce the significance of institutional spheres—religion, family, education, etc. This is a fallacy: structural differentiation helps to focus and integrate the particular competencies of a given institutional sphere; structural differentiation and role specialization reduce a given unit's responsibilities to be all things to all men. Instead of attempting to order and regulate all aspects of society, a specialized unit performs a range of key tasks within a wider, integrated system.

The process of differentiation in Latin America is blocked, weakened, and interrupted by several structural patterns other than those arising from within the Church that have deep historical roots: [3]

1. Social segmentalism, or the existence of many regional and local "societies" that attempt to be self-sufficient or politically autonomous, possessing only weak and intermittent ties with a common center: Integration and identity are bound up with ascriptive, ecological, and geographical segments, rather than with a total nation or whole society. These segments have neither the size, the structural resources, nor the legal basis for developing into differenti-

[3] These and other features of Latin American societies are described in Ivan Vallier and Vivian J. Vallier, "South American Society," David L. Sills, ed. *International Encyclopedia of the Social Sciences,* Vol. 15 (New York: The Macmillan Company & The Free Press, 1968), 68-73.

ated and viable systems, yet their very existence reduces the possibilities for more comprehensive frameworks to develop. Most Latin American nations are not integrated, functioning societies, but aggregates of segmental entities that are relatively undifferentiated within and unintegrated in terms of higher level frameworks and identities.

2. Diffuse, rather than specialized, conceptions of authority: The Latin American "leader," whether in business, politics, or religion, is viewed as a general authority and views himself as a general authority. Leadership positions are not viewed as specialized roles but as bases for articulating judgments about the whole system. The principle of limited spheres of competence is rejected in favor of concerns with diffuse power. Moreover, the chief or *jefe* is usually reluctant to delegate responsibility to subordinates. The result is a proliferation of general power roles, each of which tends to be locked into competition for the same kind of rewards. The clergy and bishops are no exception. Instead of assuming specialized roles vis-à-vis spiritual, pastoral, and ritual tasks, they are accustomed to positions as diffuse authority figures regarding politics, business, education, and the rest. One of the major problems of structural change, relatively neglected in current discourse about Latin American societies, is that of modifying conceptions of leadership roles in the direction of specialization.

3. Inclinations toward dependency on "outside help" rather than independent problem solving: Crises and goal failure tend to prompt a search for outside help, rather than focusing attention on the roots of the problem and disciplined remedial action. This pattern weakens the possibilities for specialization and structural differentiation since problem solving, at the group or collective level, usually stimulates and rewards new competencies. On the other hand, if collective crises are remedied by turning to outside help, the members of the unit are not placed under pressure to identify new competencies and make them a focus of institutionalization. Key adaptive roles are thereby thwarted and the system remains in a state of low differentiation.

CATHOLICISM AND MODERNIZATION:
A NEW PERSPECTIVE

To raise the problem of Catholicism and modernization is to touch on a long-standing scholarly controversy that has its origins in "Nineteenth-Century Studies" and more specifically in Max Weber's essay,[4] *The*

---

[4] Guenther Roth has drawn my attention to the significance of Georg Jellinek's *Die Erklärung der Menschen und Bürgerrechte* (Leipzig: Duncker & Humblot, 1895), for Weber's interests in the relationship of religious ideas to secular institutions. In a yet unpublished essay, Roth supplies a quotation from Weber's memorial address on Jellinek whereby acknowledgment is made of this influence. Guenther Roth, "Max Weber's Comparative Approach: Genesis and Maturation," Ms., 1969, pp. 10-11.

Protestant Ethic and the Spirit of Capitalism.[5] The central issue in this controversy is Weber's assertion that Protestantism and particularly the Calvinist strand played an important, though not determinant, causal role in the development of modern, bourgeois capitalism and more generally in the development of the legal, occupational, and associational principles that constitute the core of modern Western society. The Calvinist's pre-occupation with secular achievement as part of his responsibility to God and as part of his own quest for salvation engendered a "worldly asceticism," imbued secular life with deep religious meaning, and joined the routine details of everyday work to a holy concept of vocation. The aggregate effects of these pervasive orientations, i.e., "the Protestant Ethic," were at least two: a profound recasting of the principles of social order or of the premises of collective life and, second, a process of rationalization that consecutively shattered traditional social bonds and loyalties, thereby freeing motivations and resources to the extent that they could be recombined into wholly new types of enterprises.

Numerous amplifications, qualifications, and applications have been made on this general thesis.[6] Attempts have been made also to refute it. These excursions need not be summarized here, except to note that Catholicism, and Roman Catholicism more specifically, emerges as a religious system that blocks, restrains, and otherwise handicaps a country's capacities to generate and institutionalize modernizing forces. By virtue of its conceptions of religious accomplishment, its sacramental procedures for restoring religious confidence, its assent to fixed orders of hierarchical calling, and its tendency to both devalue the world and to separate ethics from mass religiosity, Roman Catholicism inclines men toward a passive acceptance of the status quo. Certain specific doctrines and beliefs also lend positive value to behaviors that work against socioeconomic change, e.g., norms governing sexual relationships in the family (the fertility problem and its demographic implications), the emphasis on charity as a noble solution to the problems of the needy (thus fixing attention on symptoms, rather than causes), and the assumption that theology stands at the apex of the educational curriculum (thus infusing many aspects of professional and technical training with religious principles). All of these

[5] George Allen & Unwin, Ltd., London, 1930, translated by Talcott Parsons.

[6] For recent developments on this thesis, see S. N. Eisenstadt, ed., *The Protestant Ethic and Modernization: A Comparative View* (New York: Basic Books, Inc., 1968), especially the following essays: S. N. Eisenstadt, "The Protestant Ethic Thesis in an Analytical and Comparative Framework," pp. 3-45; Stanislav Andreski, "Method and Substantive Theory in Max Weber," esp. 53-59 ("Catholicism and Protestantism"); Herbert Lüthy, "Once Again: Calvinism and Capitalism," pp. 87-108; and Charles and Katherine George, "Protestantism and Capitalism in Pre-Revolutionary England," pp. 155-76.

configurations help to assign Catholicism a negative role in the broad processes that go by the names of "development" and "modernization."

Does this mean that Latin American societies are doomed to hesitant and lagging patterns of change? Or is Catholicism losing sufficient degrees of influence so that newer orientations and values can gain autonomous strength and thus set these countries on their way? Perhaps neither question is particularly relevant, at least as stated. Instead, the chief problem is to assess the significance of the "new Church" for particular aspects of Latin America's developmental pattern. Some observers have already attempted this in a preliminary way. Beals,[7] for example, finds some analogies between the secular, ethical emphases of specialized Catholic Action movements and the Protestant Ethic. Sanders [8] attaches positive significance to theological developments, the growth of a more open, pluralistic conception of society and of Catholics' roles in it, the "prophetic" leadership of a growing group of Catholic elites, and the emergence of an ethical activism among laymen. Williams,[9] on the other hand, finds positive linkages between Catholicism and change within the context of progressive Christian Democratic parties. Being grounded in the religious tradition of Latin America yet oriented to change and political leadership, these parties hold a special developmental potential. However, none of these authors claims that the forces of a new Catholicism are going to have a sweeping impact on Latin America's developmental pattern.

Nor do I. The significance that I place on the emerging "new Church" draws on many of the themes that are identified by Beals, Sanders, and Williams, but from a quite different theoretical perspective. Instead of seeing direct, positive outputs flowing from manifest ideologies of change or the parallels between certain types of valued secular actions and the Protestant Ethic, I place first emphasis on the structural changes that are occurring between the Church (and its immediate institutional extensions) and the wider society. Although ideas and attitudes help to symbolize and legitimate these structural changes, they hold little importance unless new roles, new levels of interdependency, and new principles of corporate problem solving also occur and become institutionalized. Catholicism even in its modern dress is not, nor can it ever be, a second Calvinism. Nor can we suppose that if it were its consequences

[7] Ralph C. Beals, "Bureaucratic Change in the Mexican Catholic Church: 1926-1950" (Ph.D. Dissertation, University of California, Berkeley, 1966), Chapter VII, "The 'Lay Apostolate.'"

[8] Thomas G. Sanders, "Religion and Modernization" (TGS-14), Field Letter to Richard H. Nolte, Institute of Current World Affairs, New York, N. Y., August 4, 1968.

[9] Edward J. Williams, *Latin American Christian Democratic Parties* (Knoxville, Tennessee: The University of Tennessee Press, 1967), pp. 266-71.

would be the same in contemporary Latin America as they were in sixteenth and seventeenth-century Western Europe. The developmental matrix is no longer local, technologically primitive, or overshadowed with unremitting preoccupations about the hereafter. Instead the major problem is to channel and combine already existing aspirations and resources into long-range collective sequences. This means that a religion's relevance to development and modernization in low-income countries, such as Latin America, must be assessed on bases other than those that have grown out of the Weberian controversy. It is not so much a question of the individual's religious orientations but the kinds of implications corporate structures of religious control hold for the functioning of the secular power structure, for the integration of social groups, and for the stability of the general ground rules that impinge on everyday exchanges and role systems. Correspondingly, in the context of modernization, it is the kinds of responses and decisions taken by Catholic elites vis-à-vis competing value movements and secularization that make a difference. The emphasis I have given to religious competition, the industrial sector, and the political emergence of marginal groups indicates that the Church is not an independent, advanced front for change but first a follower or responder. Its importance comes, then, at the *second* and *subsequent* phases of modernization. If it confronts the emerging new forces with defensive and traditional strategies of control, the Church can significantly deflect, interrupt, and dampen their progress. On the other hand if it risks some of its prestige and leadership in favor of trying new and more specialized religious strategies, it not only releases secularly-relevant resources for further development but actually helps facilitate change.

The cases of Chile and Argentina are suggestive in these matters. Both societies have very important modern sectors, a growing industrial base, and populations with high aspirations for change and economic growth. These developments got underway in both countries during the late nineteenth and early twentieth centuries. As new groups and changing values gained ground in Chile, the Church turned toward them, demonstrated certain degrees of flexibility in revising its relationship to society, and by 1925 had accepted the separation of Church and State. Subsequently some of its leaders recognized the value of holding the Church away from direct political involvements while encouraging new ventures among progressive priests and laymen. It is not so much that the Church played a front-line role in social change but that it began to move away from institutional strategies that held a potential for thwarting secular forces already underway. The situation turned out differently in Argentina. Modernizing forces were not met flexibly and with foresight by the Church. Instead, traditional modes of defense and organization were sustained in the Church's centers, symbiotic ties between the ecclesiastical and political spheres were periodically reinforced, and innovating priests were usually throttled. I do not hold that the Church is the major source of Argentina's national problems, but had it responded differently certain strengths would have been added to forces for change.

If a Church meets the early stages of modernization by recourse to political alliances, clericalism, and confessional structures, it foments civil strife and social confusion. On the other hand, if it begins to develop itself in terms of specialized religious emphases, socioethical leadership roles, voluntary associations, and the like, then it simultaneously extricates itself from traditional involvements and frees loyalties and resources for tasks of social development. Spiritual charisma, voluntarism, and ethical influence begin to replace political power, appeals to mass emotions, and defensiveness. If this developmental sequence eventuates then the society is able to move ahead as a secular system but within the wider religious meanings of a changing Catholic tradition.

I place a great deal of weight on the decision-making capacities of Church elites, i.e., their choices, their selection of problem-solving procedures, and the things they choose to symbolize. Catholicism is still an elite system and its leaders hold independent power to set the course on many important issues of concern within the Church. Consequently I do not agree with those observers of contemporary Latin American Catholicism who hold that the Catholic masses can emerge as the forefront of the "new Church." Instead there is an increasing need for exceptional men of capable leadership who will take the initiative for accelerating the growth of the incipient and partial trends that have been identified as part of the cultural-pastoral model. They cannot alone remake Latin America but they can help invigorate, support, and symbolically express some of the positive trends that are already underway.

IMPLICATIONS FOR RESEARCH

Studies of religion and modernization will benefit considerably if more attention is given (1) to the ways in which elites and organized groups modify and develop the systemic features of the religion's control mechanisms, and (2) to the implications these initiatives or responses have for the restructuring of society. These perspectives add new variables to the causal framework, which is to say that another set of intervening variables is supplied that operates between religious beliefs and societal patterns. To date, this variable space has been covered principally by motivational models (see Figure 8.1); i.e., the individual believer, as actor, mediates between religious beliefs and secular roles.

The "system influence" model (in Figure 8.1) attaches significance to a series of heretofore neglected patterns and processes:

1. the purposive or conscious interests of religious elites as representatives of a religious tradition;

FIGURE 8.1

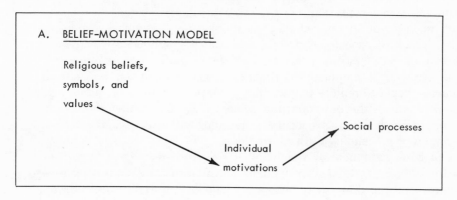

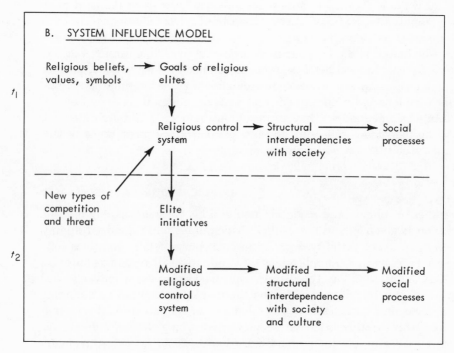

2. the capacities of such elites to alter, modify, and change their organized instruments of religious influence;

3. the sociological effects or corollaries of a religious system's organized mechanisms of influence;

4. the inevitable interpenetration and interdependence between religious structures and a society's total system of social control, power structures, and integrative base;

5. the conditions that threaten religious elites' institutionalized bases of influence and control;

6. the positive or negative implications of particular types of solutions to problems of religious control for the change and modernization of a society.

These emphases underline the necessity to recognize that religions are dynamic, changing systems, and that processes of religious change constitute fundamental aspects of the whole problem of modernization. Accordingly, the key problem in the comparative study of religion and change is not to describe the main elements of a religion's beliefs, values, and symbols and then adduce their implications for economic or political change, but to lay hold of the ways in which historical and social contexts breed structural change in a religion's characteristic systems of influence and then relate those processes to the major networks of organized influence and control in society. These patterns can then be assessed for their change implications.

All religions are led, defended, and controlled by certain elite groups and organized bodies. These basic power groups are focused on securing a position of influence in society, either through pressure-group activities, access to basic socialization roles, ideological persuasion, ritual monopolies, etc. Correspondingly, these power groups are continually defining new strategies and trying to improve the effectiveness of their various programs. These modifications may be geared to building insulative barriers against nonreligious influences or reaching new status groups. They may also be focused on acquiring new bases of religious association and cultural legitimacy.

The study of the role of Buddhism in the modernization of Southeast Asian countries, or of Islam in the Middle East, is not satisfactorily addressed by noting the formal elements of the belief system and then making inferences about the religion's obstructive or facilitative roles in social change, but by studying the structural bases of religious influence and control in society, noting the changes that are occurring, and then relating these to modernization.

Such studies are certain to be productive along several lines. First, attention is turned to the structural and institutional features of religion and society, with special possibilities for identifying types of interdependencies, power coalitions, and exchange networks. Second, the focus on changes in a religion's bases of influence and control leads directly into explanatory problems, i.e., the conditions that make for differing rates or directions of religious system change. The usual emphases on descriptive generalizations and typological exercises will be supplemented by explanatory theories. Third, policymakers and agencies that attempt to promote social change may begin to realize that religious systems are not a special and untouchable aspect of societies, but need to be made a primary focus of developmental strategies.

Index

Accion Cultural Popular (ACPO), 124
Agency for International Development (AID), 33
Alexander, Robert J., 143
Alfaro, Carlos, 18
Amazon region, 37
Anticlericalism, 21, 32, 56-59
APRA movement, 53
Apristas, 53-54
Aquinas, Saint Thomas, 22
Argentina:
  bishops in, 127
  Christian revolutionaries in, 81
  church in, 22, 122, 126-29
    systematic comparisons, 137-41
  clergy in, 126, 128
  and exercise of *patronato*, 35
  laymen in, 126, 128
  modernization and, 158-59
Autonomy, Church and state:
  established high, 35
  established low, 35
  separated high, 36
  separated low, 35

Baptism, 32, 38
Basic Education Movement (MEB), 67, 132
Beals, Ralph C., 157
Behavioral patterns, 29-32
Belgium:
  church in, 3
  episcopal conferences in, 62
Bible study groups, 70
Bilbao, Francisco, 21
Bishops, 16, 25, 39, 60, 64, 80, 93, 96, 155 (*see also* Clergy)
  administration of dioceses, 24
  in Argentina, 127
  in Brazil, 133-34
  in Chile, 89, 136, 145-46
  conservative, 79, 145
  consideration of needs of laity, 111
  cultural mutation and, 98-99
  cultural-pastoral strategy and, 69
  Little Courses in Christianity (*Los Cursillos*) and, 108

Bishops (*cont.*)
  missionary task, 37
  powers of, 15
  progressive, 2, 100, 133-34, 136, 146
    and dioceses, 100-101
  role of, 37, 86-88
  and seminaries, 100
  and socioethical leadership, 85, 88, 119
  traditionally oriented, 91
  in United States, 94
Bogota, 123
Bolatti, Bishop Guillermo, 127
Bolivia, 67, 122
Brazil:
  Amazon region, 37
  Basic Education Movement (MEB) in, 67, 132
  bishops in, 133-34
  Catholic Action movements in, 65
  Christian Democratic party in, 92-94
  Christian revolutionaries in, 81, 137
  church in, 21, 122, 131-34
    systematic comparisons, 137-41
  clergy in, 131-33
  dioceses in, 134
  laymen in, 131-32
  missionary work in, 37
  Pentecostals in, 143-44
  political movements in, 94
  priests in, 33
  radical movements in, 58
British Isles, Roman Catholicism in, 147
Bruneau, Thomas C., 133
Buddhism, 161
Buenos Aires, 127, 139

Calvinism, 156-57
Camara, Dom Helder, 2, 132-33
Canada, episcopal conferences in, 62
Canon law, 15
Caro Rodríguez, José María, 145-46
Casas, Bartolomé de las, 51
Catholic Action movements, 66, 80, 93, 107, 109, 113, 119, 129, 157
  in Brazil, 65
  in Chile, 65
  general, 64, 73
  and laymen, 64
  rural, 67
  specialized, 64, 73

B'

2